Loves Lost

and Found

Loves Lost and Found

by Michael Ray King

illustrated by Tracy McDurmon

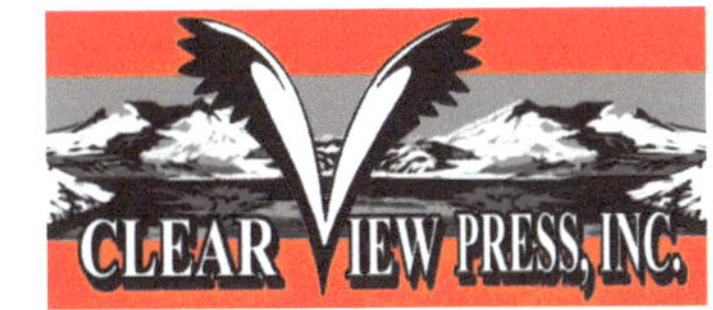

ClearView Press, Inc., Palm Coast, FL

Loves Lost and Found
Cover Design by BT Graphics. All rights reserved.
Photography of Paintings by Scott Dinglefelder. All rights reserved.
Copy Editor Beth Mansbridge
Copyright © July 2009 by Michael Ray King & Tracy McDurmon

King, Michael Ray
McDurmon, Tracy

ISBN 978-0-9799623-1-8

LCCN 2009907009

All Rights Reserved. No part of this book may be reproduced, stored in a retrieval system, or transmitted in any form or by any means, electronic, mechanical, photocopying, recording, or otherwise, without permission in writing from ClearView Press, Inc.

ClearView Press, Inc.
PO Box 353431
Palm Coast, FL 32135-3431
clearviewpressinc.com

Printed in the United States of America

I pondered quite a while as to whom I would dedicate my part in this endeavor, and I kept coming back to why I began this journey in the first place, which led me to a time in my life a few years previous. For my own reasons I won't mention any names. They will know who they are when they read this and that's what matters.

This person touched my life in such a profound way that I was to change the direction of my life completely. I had just been through hell and hadn't realized my full potential yet as an artist, but had always dreamed of putting my art out there for others and for myself.

This person said one simple sentence, not knowing the impact it would have on me. I'm sure they will be surprised by this. They said, "Don't ever change what you do best." At the time I hadn't changed what I did best; I just hadn't given it my best shot.

I dedicate my labor of love in this book to that person, who to this day reminds me of how we all affect each other—for good and bad—how we constantly struggle to live up to our potential, how we should love with all our heart, and how sometimes we get lost.

Thank you for reminding me all is not lost.

All my Love,

Tracy

To Pat, who handed me a dream,

and

Tracy, who helped make one come true.

Michael Ray King

Contents

Foreword – Tracy McDurmon

Within these pages lies an artistic woman's interpretational vision of a man's innermost thoughts and feelings on the subject we call Love. Whether that love was helpful or hurtful at the time, it was expressed and has found its way into our rendition of ***Loves Lost and Found***. I took this opportunity as a challenge, to see what I could envision from Mike's poetry. The poetry brought up a lot of my own emotions in the "love" area, and at one point I thought myself unable to conquer this project. With time, I found myself intrigued as to what some men think and feel about love.

Reading through this collection of verse, you too will see that deep down inside—and I say "real deep"—introspective men really do feel as women do when it comes to love; they just don't go around expressing it the same way. Then I realized that many women tend to keep emotions buried as well. Here we offer our version of the uncovering of those natural, lucid feelings and thoughts. I wish we all shared them more often. Let the images sweep you away. I want to thank Mike for his "love" and support. Let's clone him!

Love and light,
Tracy McDurmon

Foreword – Michael Ray King

This project, ***Loves Lost and Found***, actually birthed in autumn 1982. I had written quite a bit of poetry and wanted to have it illustrated and put in a book format as a Christmas gift for family and friends. Money was tight, so I attempted to create the illustrations myself. To say the least, it was a naïve effort, but one I cherished.

Fast-forward to the summer of 2008: I mentioned this age-old project to Tracy at a writers' group meeting. One thing led to another and before I knew it, we were embarked on a "labor of love" project. ***Loves Lost and Found*** was born over the next six months. Tracy's art introduced me to the fascinating field of interpretive painting.

Tracy has a signature style that defines her work. I love to pop in and check out whatever painting she's working on at the moment. I am grateful to have crossed paths with her, and I look forward to many more opportunities to see her work displayed. You are in for a visual treat.

As for the poetry, most of it was penned in Raleigh, North Carolina, in the early 1980s. These were tumultuous times in my life, and many people have suggested I should put these writings out for public consumption. My hope is that something in these poems touches your life and, if nothing else, allows you to feel you are not alone in some of your emotional turmoil.

Tracy selected these poems from about one hundred. Four of the poems, in the center of the book, I decided to include after the paintings were completed. I sincerely hope you enjoy our "labor of love."

Peace and love,

Michael Ray King

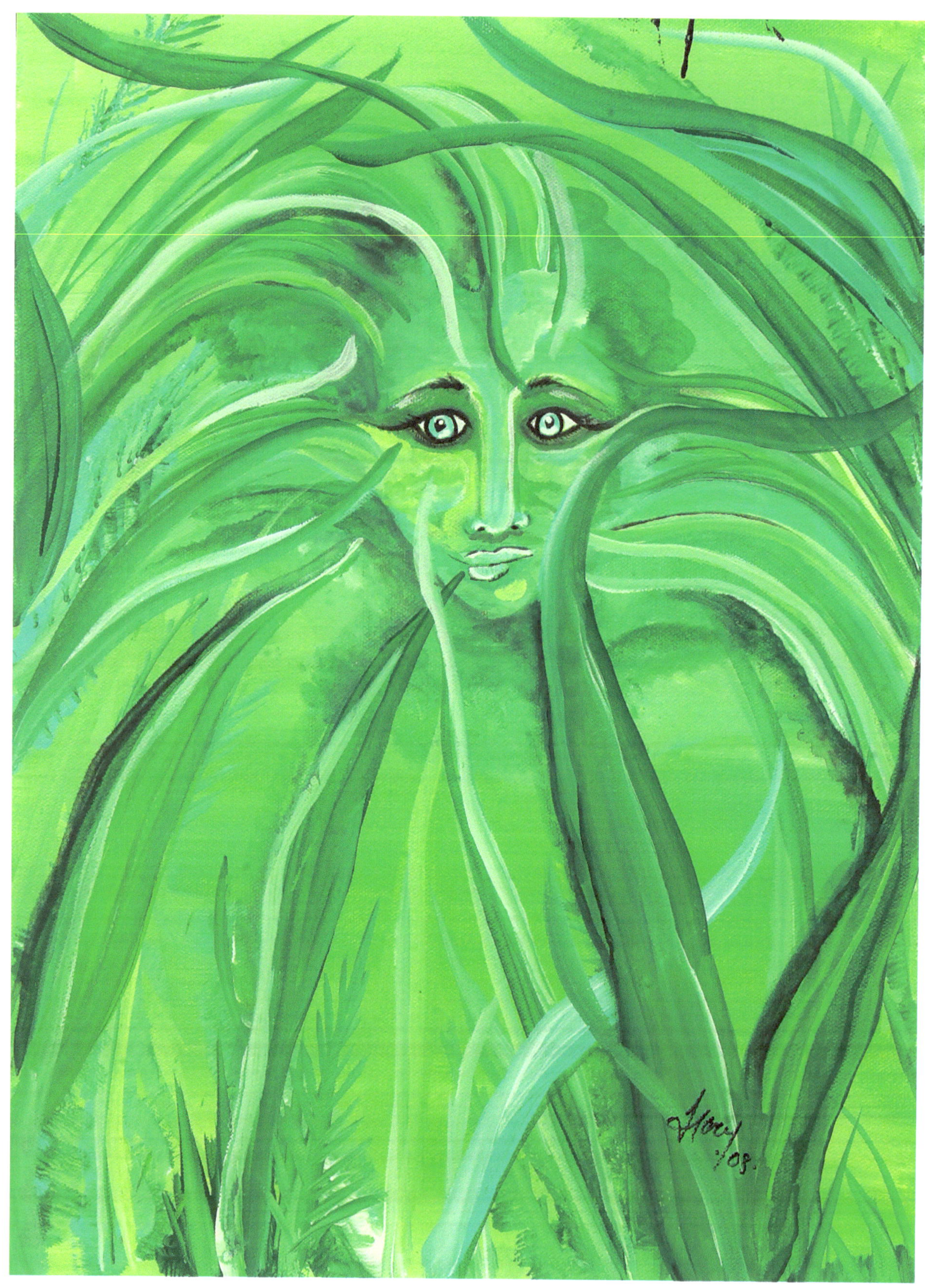

Rendezvous

Rendezvous

I sat,

Waiting for the trees to dance.

Leaves filled the air with their tuneful romance.

Wind swept my ears this night in haunting fury.

Mind at its rest, no need to hurry.

A moment,

Recaptured from days in my youth.

Feeling life in my lungs,

Hearing it whisper through the trees …

Over the pond …

Then I lost it,

It was gone.

Life and I,

We meet now and then,

When I am alone.

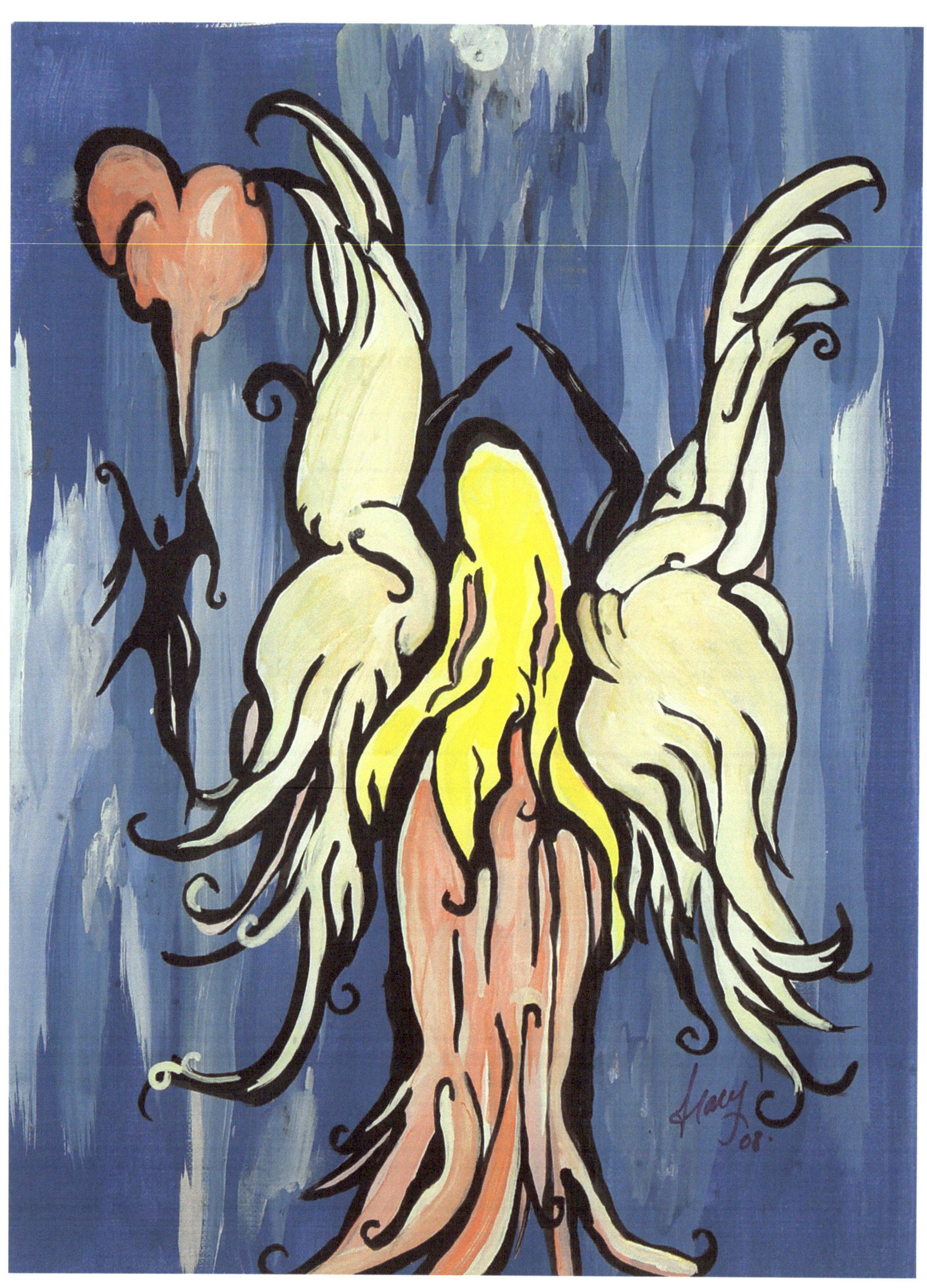

Pastel Angels

Pastel Angels

Loneliness and solitude
Are all we ever have,
When days make us strangers
And nights blind our ways.
We look forward to happier days.

My pen can reach
No further than my dreams.
My heart can feel
No more than is there.

Pastels of two angels
Are visions of a dream,
The pictures themselves
May be more than they seem.

Losing could be so tragic.

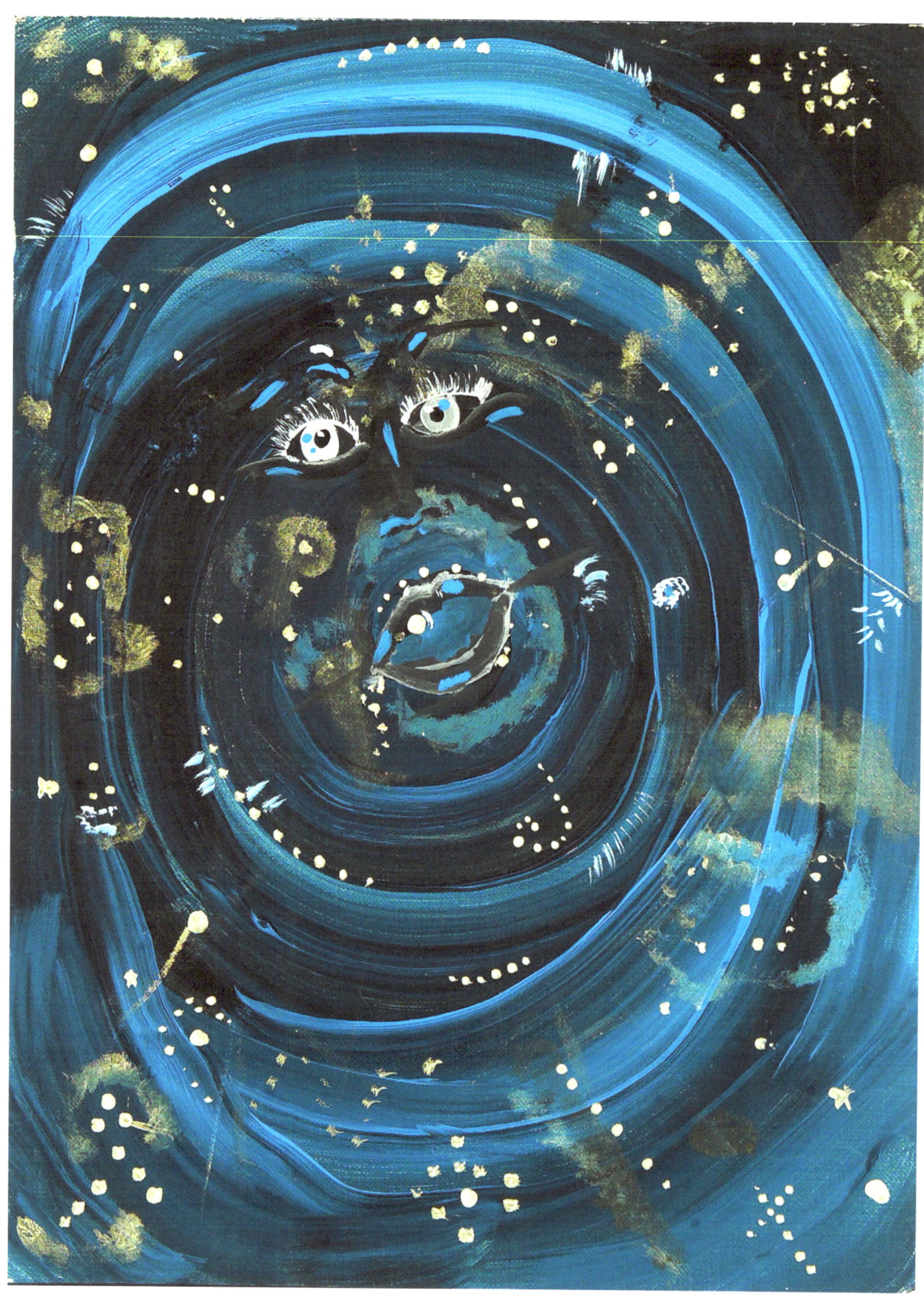

View from the Top

View from the Top

We are self-made egos.

Consciences devoid of consciousness.

Self-praising souls, absent from reality.

Fools, toying with our own minds.

We are egotists. Misrepresenting truth,

not only to others, but ourselves as well.

Liars in the land of make-believe,

where all is as said, and all is not truth.

We are egomaniacal,

gawking from our universe-centered opinions,

we see everything but ourselves.

We see nothing …

of importance.

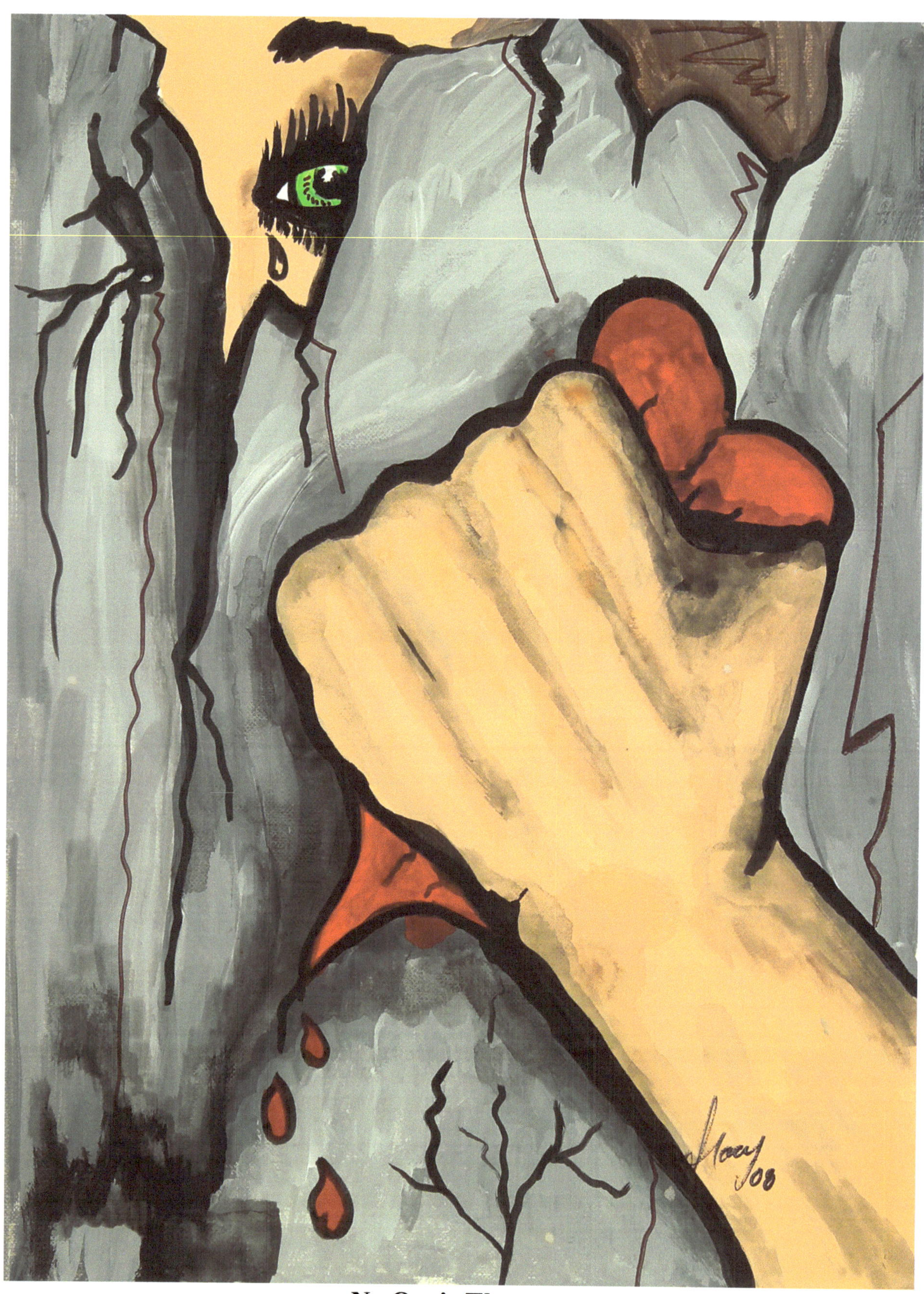

No One's There

No One's There

Alone is not so lonely as
not having a life to share

It is not so bad as one may think
until it's thought that no one's there

Except you, a room and empty dreams
in which only you believe

And the person sitting behind the pen
is the only one deceived

How frail emotion makes a man
is such a humbling slap

When life comes crumbling inward
falling ever in your lap

Sorting out the shards of love
in search of inner peace

Acquiring only cuts and gouges
the likes of which may never cease

You suffer from within yourself
wanting to show you really care

And it's not as bad as one may think
until it's thought that no one's there

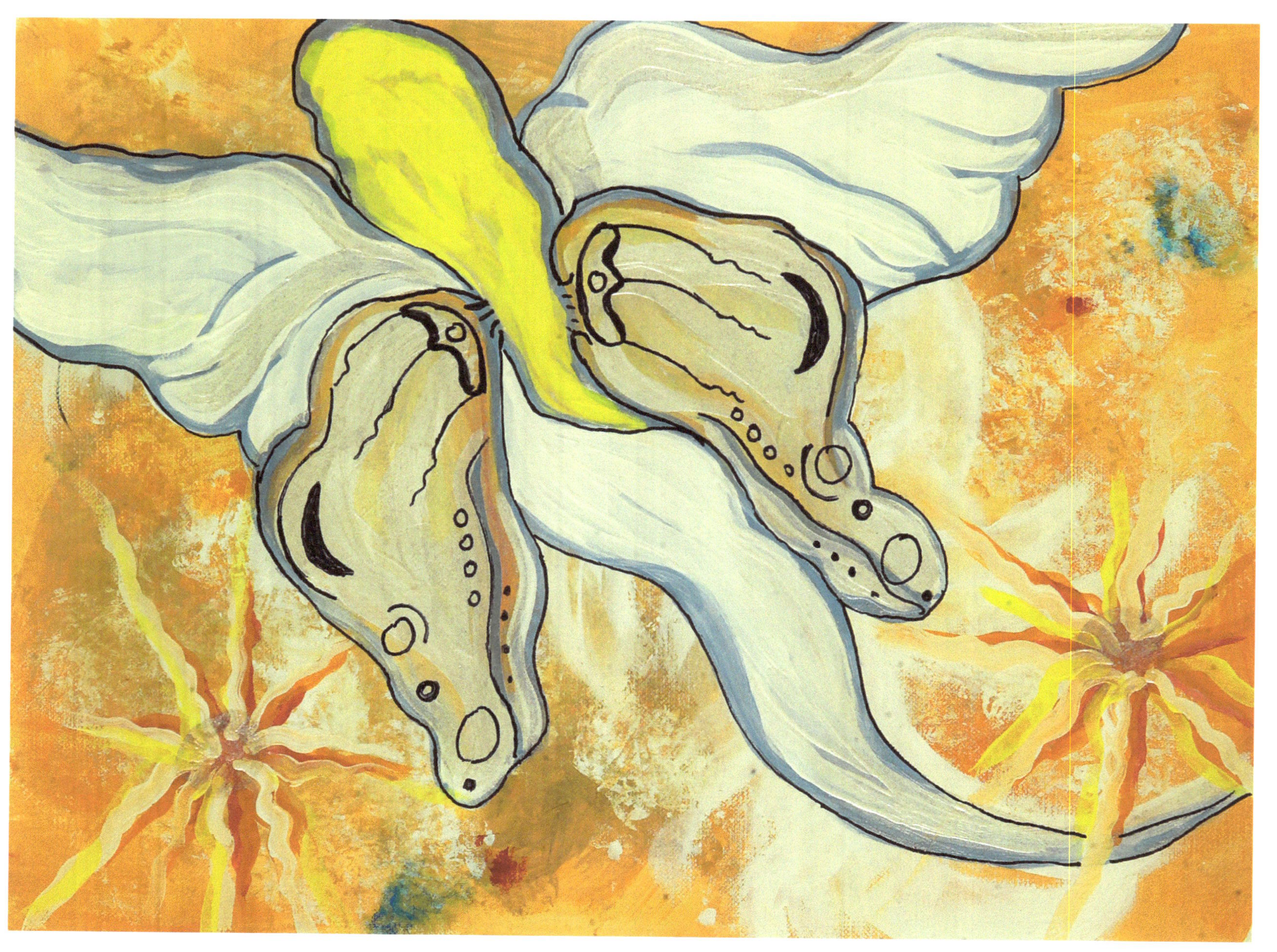

A Little Advice

A Little Advice

Wish on a star
Pray in the night
Walk in the shadows
Strive for the light

Want more from life
Than most can achieve
Embrace patience with love
And strive to believe

As night falls around you
Hear the sounds of life
Fear nothing unseen
Be happy tonight

Feel the sunset
Believe in the dawn
Remember tomorrow
Forever moves on

Love walks in the Tarheel night
Trees sing and shadows fall
With a stroll in these forests
Your peace you'll recall

Smug trees, wind's mysteries
They know what we seek
Discover their secret
Learn how to peek

Stretch with the evening
Relax with the night
See with your senses
Your future is bright

After a while, all becomes simple

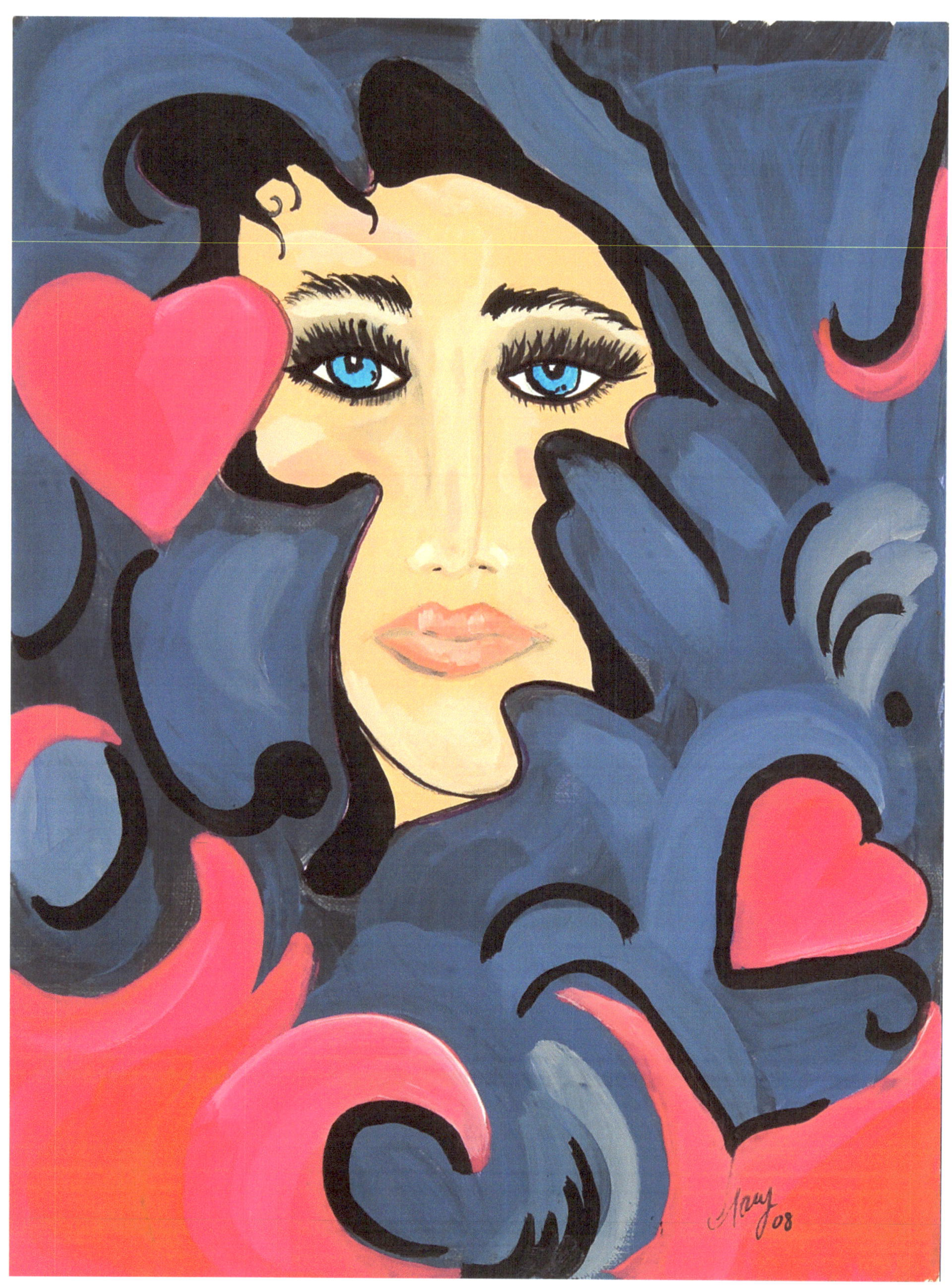

Love's Blue Blood

Love's Blue Blood

White pages before my eyes

Escape of sleep is all I care for.

That is not entirely true.

If I did not care for anything

Escape would be unnecessary.

I shall bleed over this white page

Cold, blue blood that carries my heart

From its encasement in lead, where no one ever sees

To this bandage that serves only to disinfect the wound.

"Forget all your troubles, ignore them with me!"

It usually works, I lie there and hope

That tonight's dream will end as I wish my life to begin,

A cheap therapy that only passports the pain

Into the next barrier—tomorrow's domain.

Why did I rhyme just now?

So far it's been prose.

The rhythm I am fighting

So as to lengthen my thoughts.

Alas, I have strayed from my wound and the bleeding,

Freezing my heart while still actually needing

To talk and to say straight to your heart

I love you.

I wish you could love me.

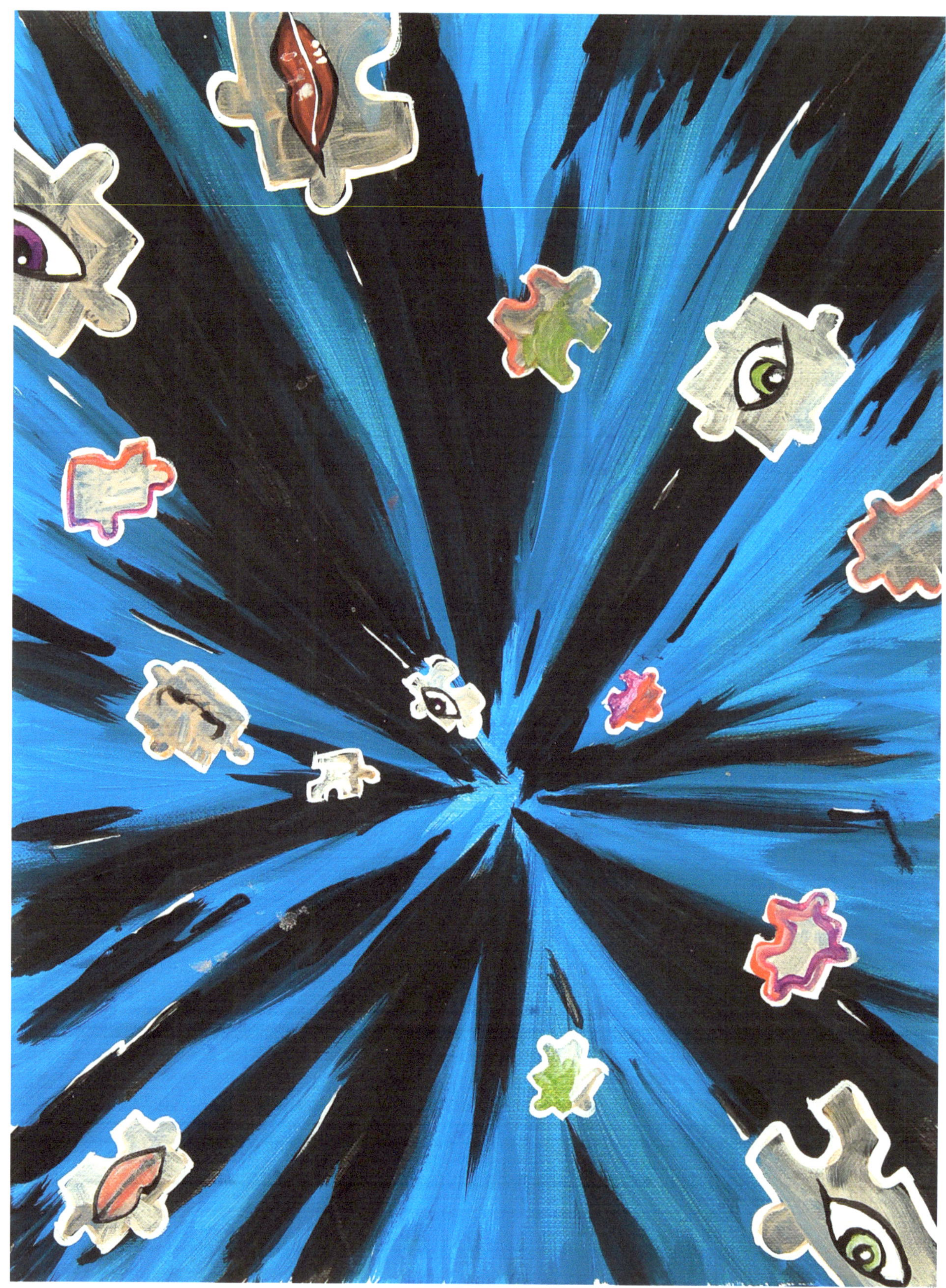

Mind Blown

Mind Blown

You are so self-destructive.
Your own explosion in your personal war.
You fragment and fly off in all directions,
Anger and frustration channeled into your mind,
Making the craziness all the more insane,
Making the loneliness all the more devastating,
Making your loveless life all the less lovely.

You are so self-destructive,
Not believing in dreams.
Why seriously live when you have nothing to hope for?
Is that what you are doing?
Occupying space and time until you die?
Are these not the reasons you weep alone?
Oh, you may not cry out loud,
But you do in your soul.

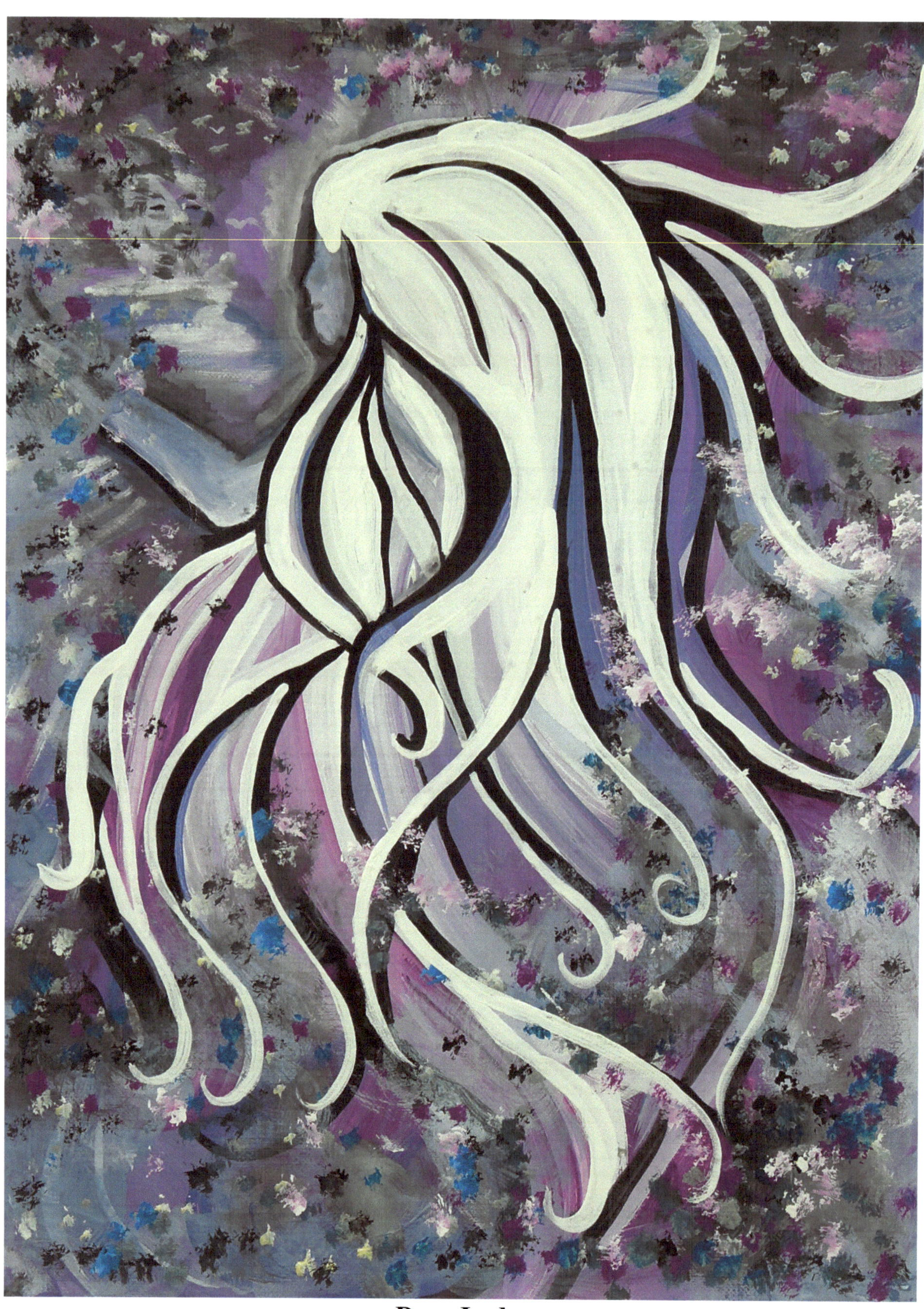

Dear Lady

Dear Lady

In the quiet solitude of this warm evening
I wish you were here
Yet I feel so safe and warm knowing
I've nothing to fear

I hear your voice
My heart drowns in joy
Seems I keep babbling
Like a nervous young boy

You don't seem to mind
You let it all slide
I bare my feelings
There's nothing to hide

When we kiss
It's like nothing before
Keeps me wanting
So very much more

Dear lady, I don't know
What I should do
I'm playing by ear
I'm playing it true

I've fallen in love
I hear your fear
But from here
Deep from within
There's nothing to lose
So much to win

If I did nothing
But cry in the night
Let the emotion
Tie me up tight
It could do me no worse
To say what I feel
To show you my heart
Is truly for real

Then if all fails
If all is denied
I won't have to feel
Like I never had tried

You are so gorgeous
So quiet, so kind
So full of quick laughter
So sharp of mind

Your smile is so pretty
Your eyes are so sweet
Your face is totally
A visionary treat
Its beauty and texture
So graphic and warm
Each time I see it
The emotion's reborn

I could trace your eyebrows
The curve of your cheeks
With fingers enchanted
For infinite weeks

I fall in your eyes
Drawing ever closer
There's nothing stopping us
From kissing forever

To be lost in your beauty
To be one, hand in hand
Together all evening
One woman, one man
Sharing the moments
Of wondrous bliss
We look at each other
We know we must kiss

There's no other option
No other play
It's obvious both of us
Want it that way
We struggle for answers
We don't get and then
We see the inevitable
Together again

This may not be so inevitable
Pure wishful thinking from me
That's just something
You must expect to see
Because I feel
We are a wonderful pair
That beauty's around
whenever you're there

I wished I was yours
Last night in my dreams
We walked in a valley
Crossed clear running streams
You held me so close
I lost my mind
You spoke to me quietly
You're incredibly kind

My heart spoke up
In its cheeriest voice
"You know this young lady
Is sure quite the choice!"

Choice? I say!
Where have you been?
It isn't as though
I pulled her from ten

I know my heart
Stands up and sings
Of the joy that my
Lady friend brings

I'm glad for the evenings
We've spent together
I'm glad for the chance
Things may even get better

I'm glad for our time
Feelings so new
I'm glad in this world
There is a wonderful you

Sincerely,
From me to you

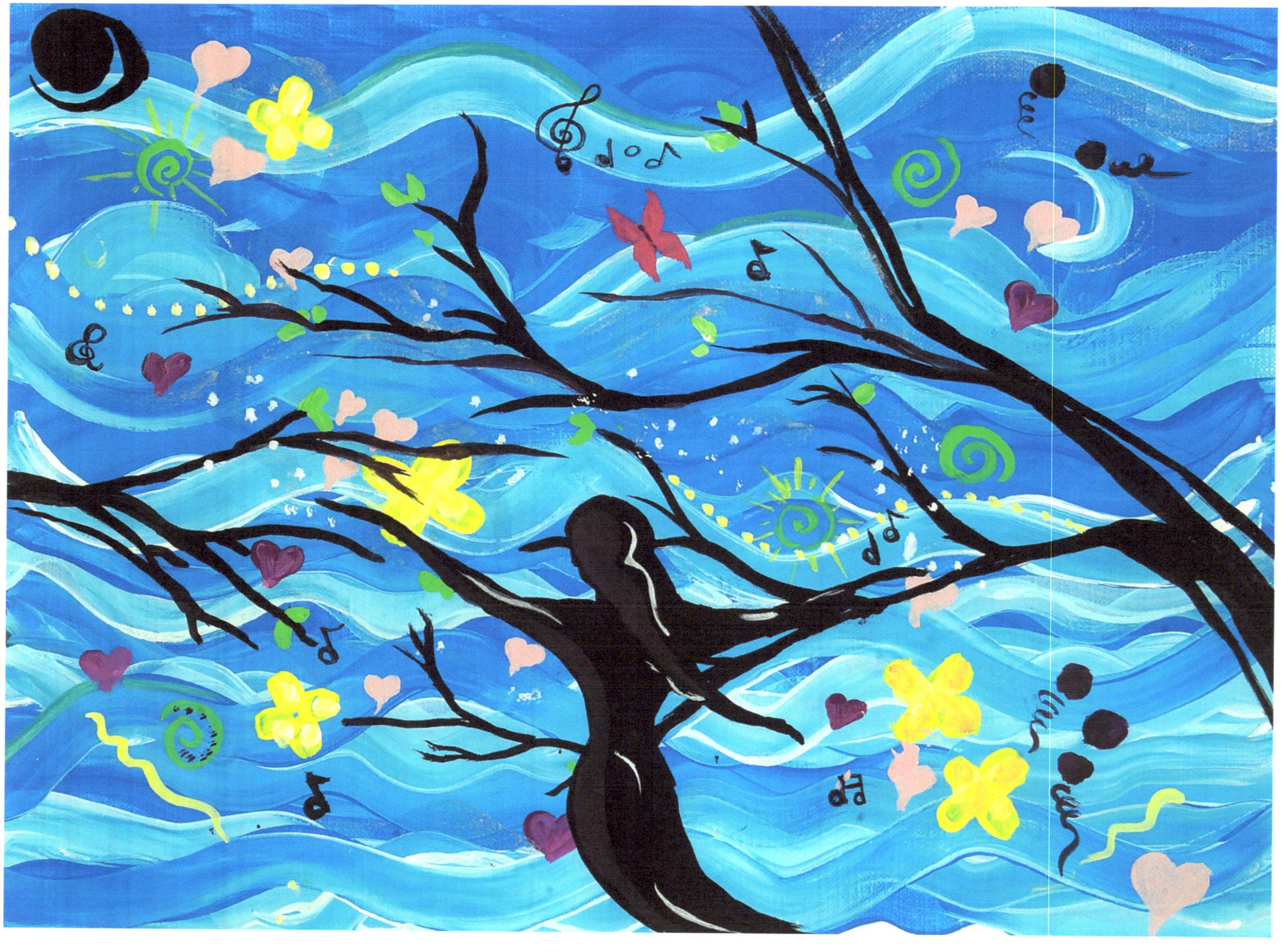

Melody of a New Dawning

Melody of a New Dawning

Good morning, life, and how are you?
It's been such a very long time.
I've missed out on your best so far,
I have come to claim what's mine.

Hello, dreams! Where've you been?
I've waited much too long.
Your colors and hue have always been true,
I want to fully belong.

Spring has delivered a reverie,
A song of flowers and trees.
Life has brought back the melody
The music of the birds and the bees.

It is a melody!
Of a beautiful new dawning.
A song to live and to breathe.
Charting high above the branches,
Dreams return my life to me.

Good morning, life! I'm doing fine!
It has been such a long, long time.
I'll not miss out on your best again,
Because now I know what is mine.

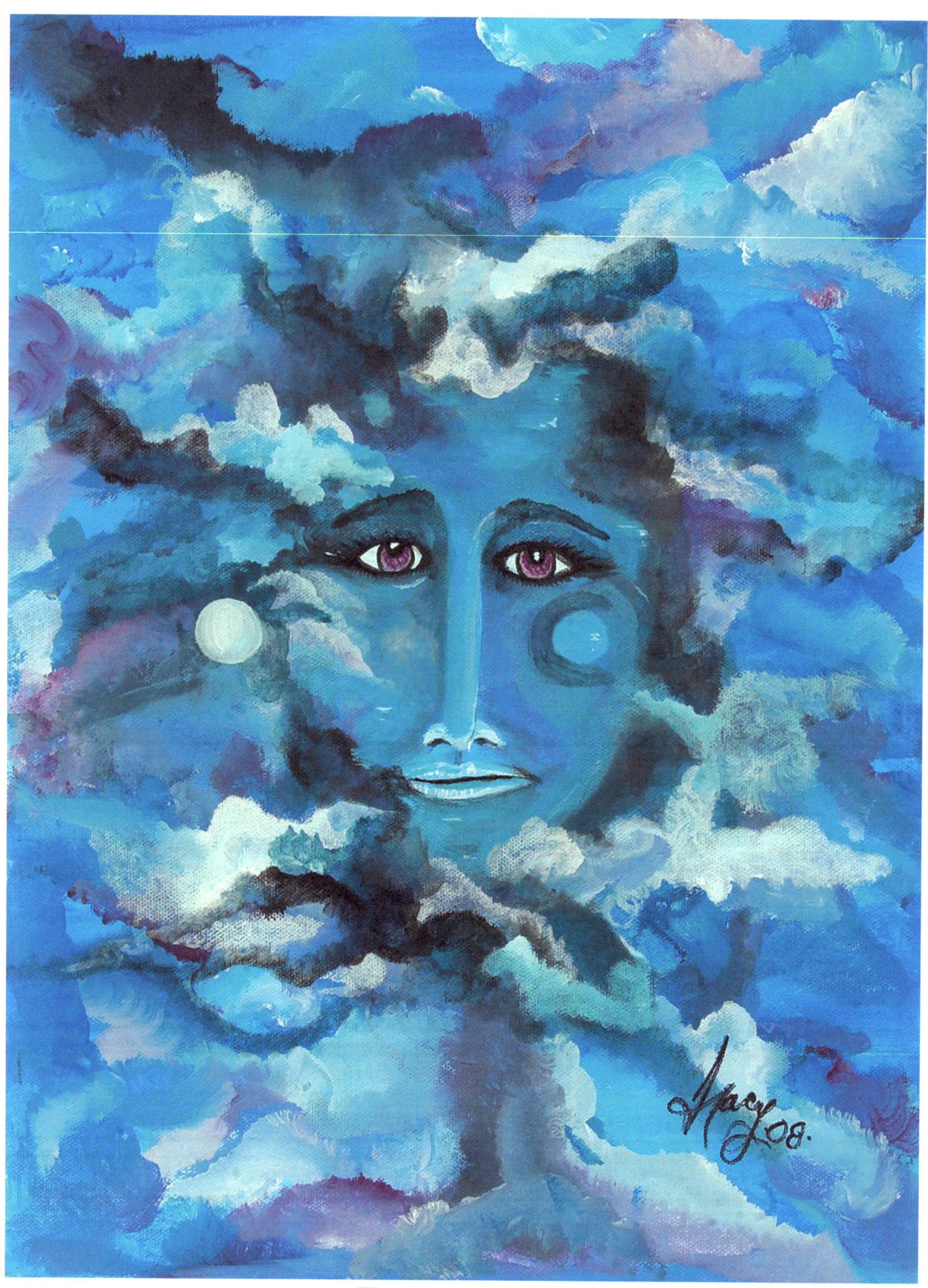

The Last Moon

The Last Moon

Love's shadows, wavering mists of life,
Phantoms that tease temporal souls.
Wind wisps frolicking over mankind, endless and without a care,
Until that night, the night of the last moon.

Black, yet illumined by the heavenly realm,
Days of man plummet headlong into the night of no recovery.
Night of the last moon shows tides that sing glory
Night of the last moon lends a crown to man's story.

In the night of the last moon
All peace is not won
But forged by death's knocking
No wars for want of armies, no death for want of life.

The last moon rules over the Earth
A beacon to no avail
The last moon rules the heavens
The last moon to gaze upon Earth means peace has come at last.

Et Tu, Bruté?

Whispers over telephone lines,
Secrets in the dark
Battle plans and serpentine talk,
Watch out for their minds!

Rendezvous and clandestine meetings,
Foreplay in the park
Touching, groping, and some climactical hoping,
Et tu, Bruté? Let me go!

Et tu, Bruté?
One day I'll understand
Why I sit and waste away,
For the sake of another man.

Et tu, Brenda, it is alright,
You really meant no harm.
You fell to the pressure of his talk,
(I bet you used your charm!)

Whispers died into regular speech,
My part faded so quickly.
Wedding bells and sweet little girls,
You both are welcome to hell!

Et tu, Bruté,
The day is here, I understand,
I am living life that is full and free,
While you die by your very hand.

Et tu, Brenda? I am alright,
You really did no harm.
You fell to the pressure of his talk,
(What a waste of charm!)

Another's Warming

Chasing dreams of futures passed,
Glancing over a windowsill,
I see a vision in my heart,
Soon it will be gone.

She rose on the horizon
As a bright idea to me.
Not knowing she was frozen,
Temperature is so hard to see.

Water runs and batters walk,
When they really should be dancing.
My vision dies in the twilight air,
At the hand of another's warming.

One day I will wear a crown of glory,
Be some child's bedtime story.
But for now I watch and wait,
For the dream to exit a lonely gate.

A new dawn rises all too soon,
Breaking in another day,
While I wait in the midnight air,
Willing my vision to pass away.

We had to run before we walked,
We had no time for dancing.
She rides away in the morning air,
On the hand of …
Another's warming.

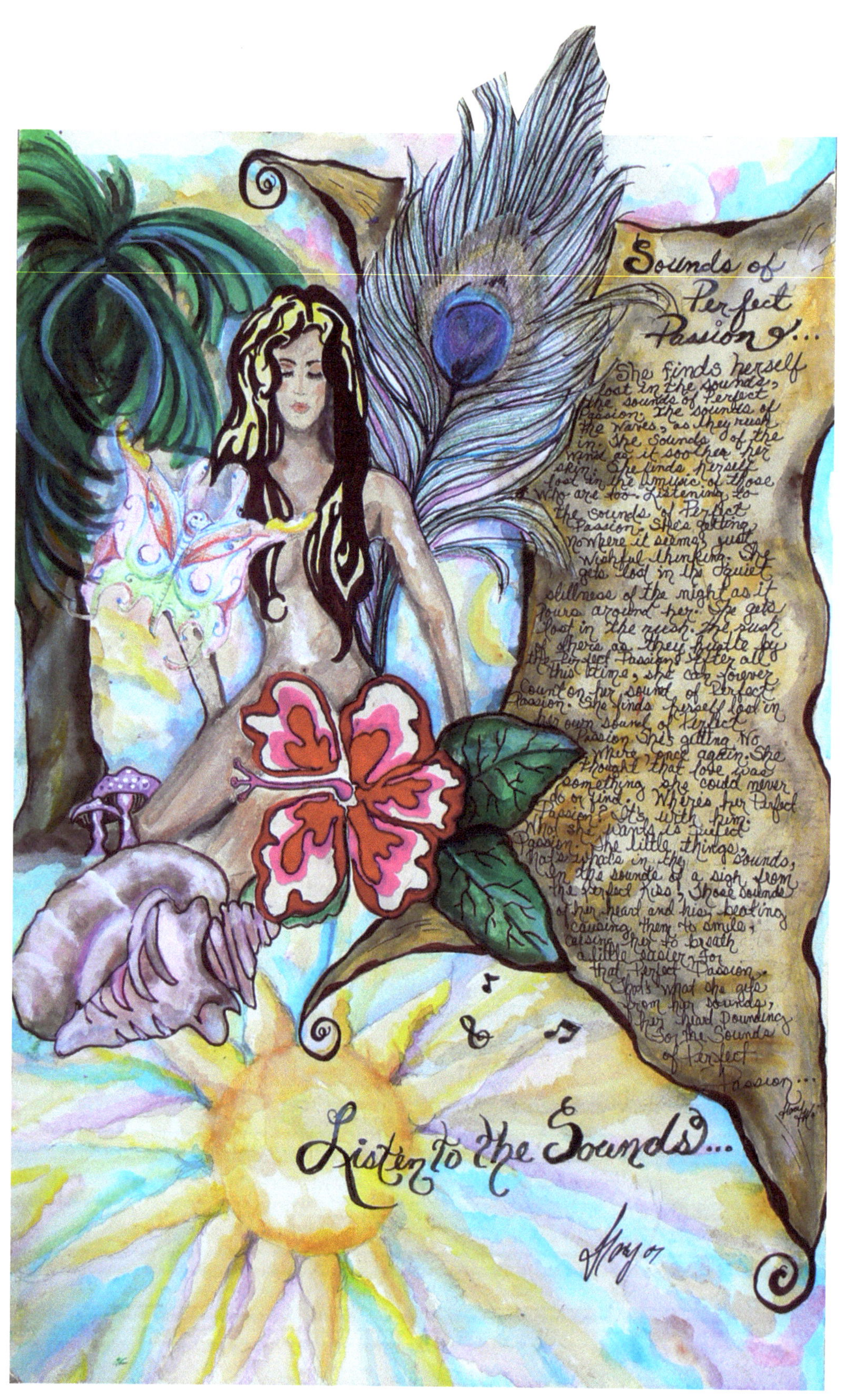

Sounds of Perfect Passion

Sounds of Perfect Passion

She finds herself lost in sounds,

The Sounds of Perfect Passion.

The sounds of the waves as they rush in,

The sounds of the wind soothing her skin.

She finds herself lost in the music of those who are, too,

Listening to the Sounds of Perfect Passion.

She's getting nowhere, it seems; just wishful thinking.

She gets lost in the stillness of the night as it pours around her.

She gets lost in the rush, the rush of others hustling by the Perfect Passion.

After all this time she can forever count on her Sound of Perfect Passion.

She finds herself lost in her own Sound of Perfect Passion.

She's getting nowhere once again.

She thought that love was something she could never do or find.

Where's her Perfect Passion? It's with him.

What she wants is Perfect Passion.

The little things, that's what's in the sounds:

In the sounds of a sigh from the Perfect Kiss, those sounds of her heart and his,

Beating, causing them to smile, causing her to breathe a little easier, for that Perfect Passion.

That's what she gets from her sounds, her heart pounding for the

Sounds of Perfect Passion …

Tracy McDurmon

Love Is Female in Gender

Water in a rippling pool,
New-fallen rain, wind blowing cool.
Rampaging fires of love and longing,
Reach up from depths for want of belonging.

Mysterious lady, you control the night,
With your veils of fancy, evasion of light.
You walk in the shadows, you skirt through the room.
Where is your black cat? Where is your broom?

Bracelets of silver fall at your wrists.
Shadows and darkness your prerequisites.
I know what I want, I know it is you.
Won't you give me your love? Give me what's due?

I chase her down alleys and find that my feet
Cannot keep the pace, cannot keep the beat.
I really do crave her, and, do I dare?
Allow myself to feel I really do care?

That's when she has me, that's when she'll turn.
That's when I catch her, that's when I burn.
I knew what I wanted, I knew it was you.
Did I get what I asked for? Or did I get what was due?

Love is female in gender.
Maybe that's why love is so tender.
It is definitely why love is so cruel.
She brings you her mystery.

She leaves you a fool.

The World Today

Ideas are lost

where victories are won,

freedoms relinquished

under threat of the gun.

Love is squandered

by those who have none.

Is this any way to live?

Or die?

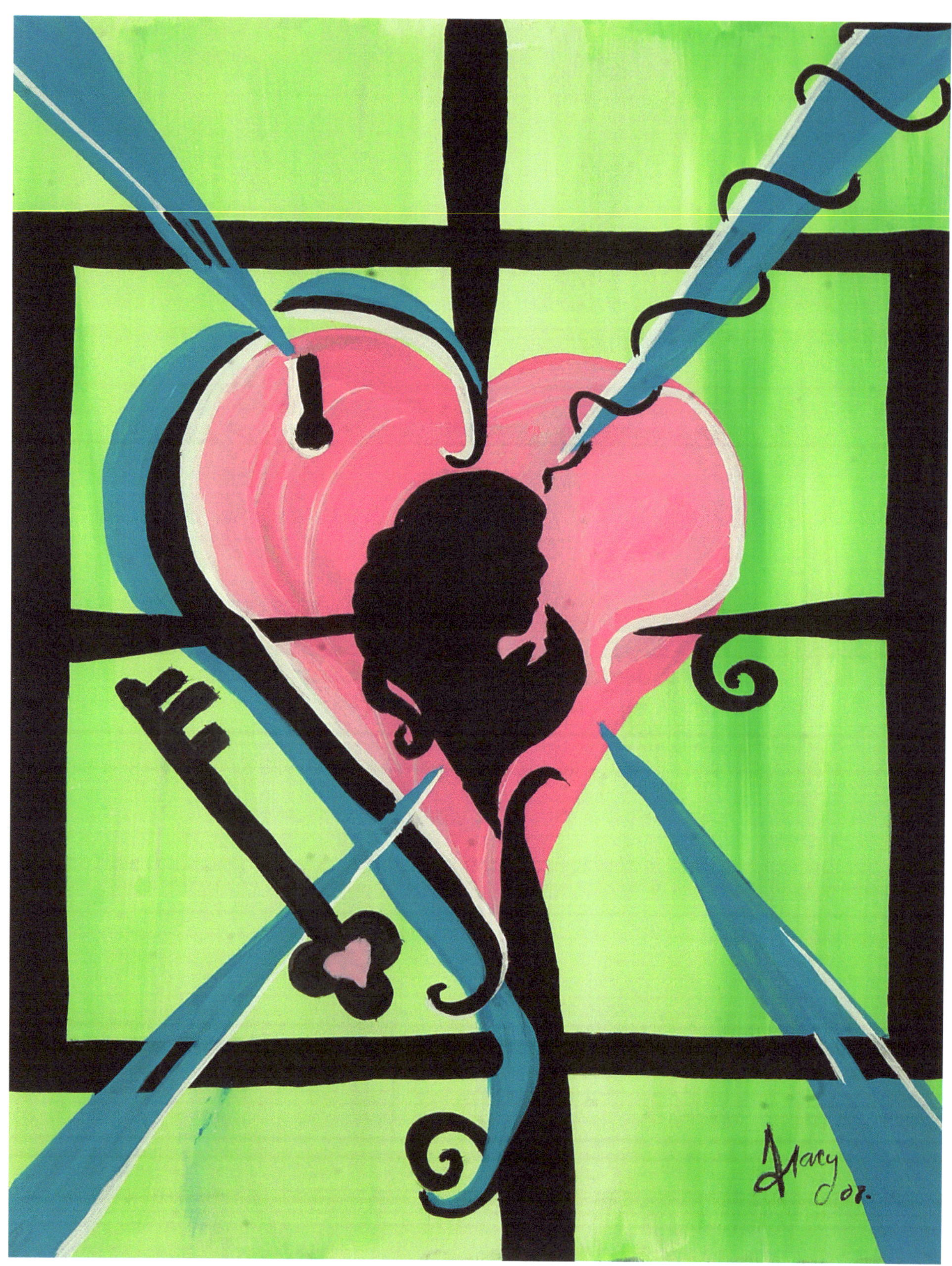

The Window

The Window

Today I saw you in my heart.
You often make your presence felt,
standing before the personal window to my soul.

There you were, simply standing.
You knew I could see you.
You're the only one who knows where I look from within my heart.

I saw clearly why I love you.
Not for any one reason,
I saw honesty first.
No makeup, no pretense, no absolute promises
other than you will always be in my heart.

I saw anarchy and a tempestuous insistence on doing as you please,
while honoring the commitments you have made in life.
I observed a walking contradiction,
but you were standing statue still.
You were standing so still you became a question.

What questions would you ask of me?
Can I accept this honesty?
Can I love you, who may never be mine?
Can I allow you to run within my heart, free access, no supervision?
Can I afford to love you?

I looked out my one-way window,
knowing that it is unfair,
observing from this high-ground view.

I must walk through a locked door to reach you.
While I can break it down, I wish not to,
my door to you is about all that is left when it comes to love.

I need you to unlock it, I have no key.
You are there.
You alone. No one else allowed.
Unfortunately others will see what you do if you unlock it.
Immobility is safe for both of us.
You can let me out whenever you like,
I do not ever want to be a burden,
hence my reluctance to break it down.
I am ready.
I realize you may never be.

Even so, you have already given me more than I may ever see again.
Honesty may not be beautiful all the time,
but it is admired and loved within my heart.
Your footsteps echo throughout the halls,
bouncing off the many, many walls,
finding their way back to me in my window,
causing me to look out to find you in the darkness.

Hearing these echoes helps me find you when I need you.
When you sleep, I have such dreams!
When you tire, I walk with a heavy heart.
I guess you could say you are the caretaker.
I am ultimately responsible for myself,
but over the many years,
you have become my best of all possible worlds.

My goal in life, my hope for life,
is when I see you again this quiet, Monday night.
A single star in my sky, white chiffon clouds misting my view.
Yet I know the clarity you give me in front of my window,
and I wish out to you, over this great expanse,
to come to me and say "I love you."
Not for my sake or knowledge, but for us, you and me,
to meet in that doorway and embrace,
to kiss an eternal kiss of honest love
between a man and a woman.

I feel I have your key and I am ready to use it.
No doubt you have mine.
We need to use them together, though we may never get the chance.
I know this.

Interesting that our keys open the same door but with differing locks.
Knowing us, it could really be no other way.
If nothing else, I wish you to know, see, hear,
feel, and touch this final thought
with every fiber of your consciousness.
I see you standing before my window
in the refuge I built from a cold world.
Baring yourself of pretense,
you offer honesty as your only possession.
While you may see it this way too, the truth is that you own
the halls you echo through,
not because you stole or bought them,
but simply because I have given them to you.

As was true in my impetuous youth, my love is yours,
no strings attached.
Come unlock the door anytime.
We will spend our lives together.
I love you.

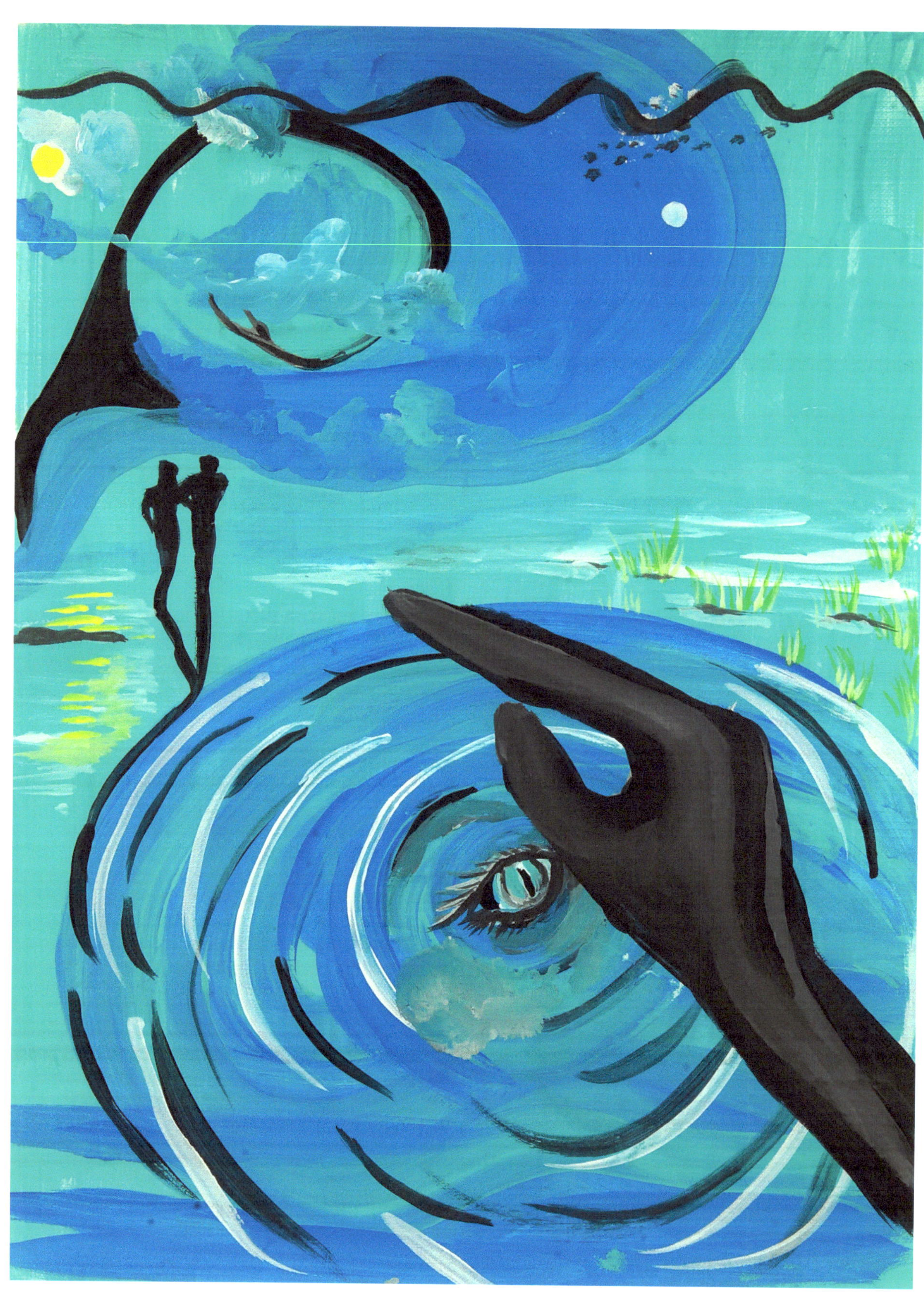

Hold Life by the Hand

Hold Life by the Hand

See the lover clasp together,
Watch them ripple in the waves.
Sigh at the moon high above
Listen to the evening slip away.

Hear the sound of a thousand crickets,
Feel the coolness of the air.
Touch the grass on which you are lying,
Sense the joy of being there.

Realize the beauty of the sunrise,
Know that it is grand.
Be in awe of a magnificent sunset,
And hold life by the hand.

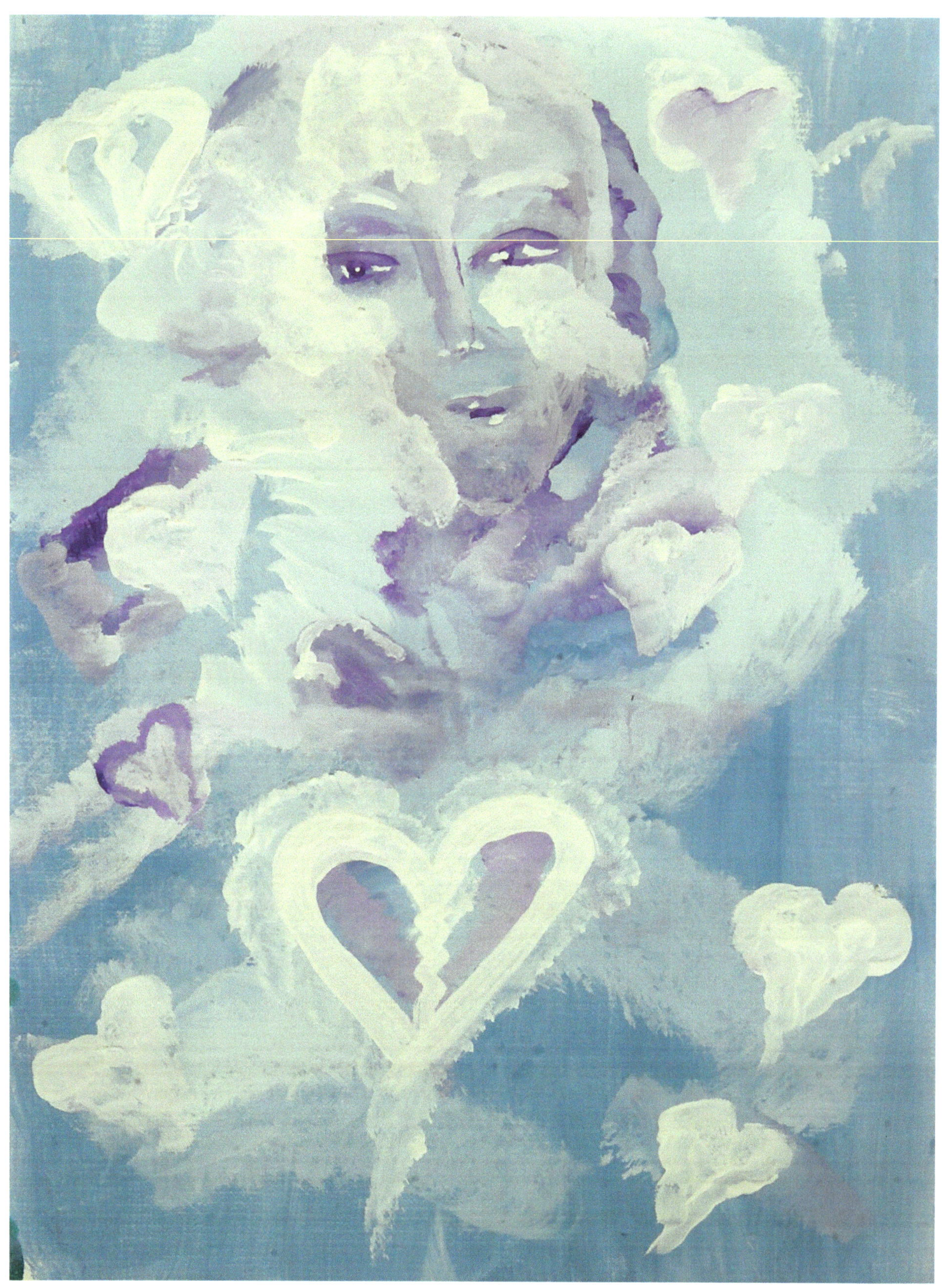

Leaving

Leaving

Turmoil days trample passion
Harsh word days grind the heart
Unkindness sears the soul
All that's left is hollow and hurt

Chest void, head dead
Spirit lost to space unoccupied
Tears reject the call
Desire spikes from desperation

Door opens, a purple butterfly smiles and
Carries shadows of pain away with
Faces in the wings, floating cares to the wind
Leaving was critical.

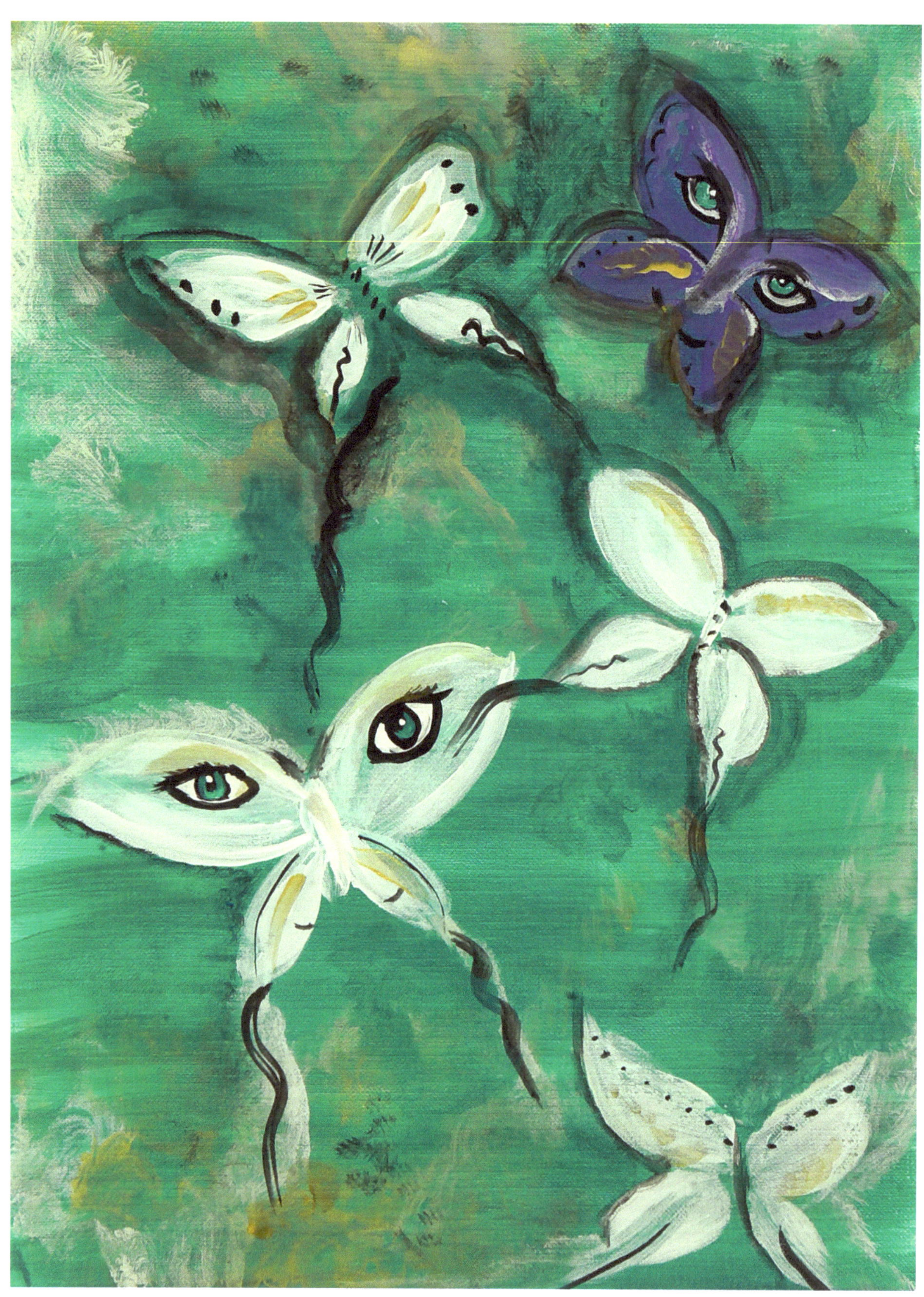

How Many Times?

How Many Times?

How many times can one return to his childhood home?
How many times can he look upon those playgrounds of old,
Full of such happy memories of friends, days, and events gone by?

How many times can he return to the old visions, still intact?
Too often the return is made to a place once beautiful, now decrepit,
Or once decrepit and believed to always remain so, now beautiful.

Possibly most disconcerting is to return to the same tree, the same fence,
As if untouched by time and circumstance.
To sit there and softly remember, to smell the air as a child once again,
To feel the heat of the sun as nonchalantly as in those early years,
And then to remember his first love.

How many times will he think of her and wish, If only …
How many times will sadness and regret cross his mind
At thoughts of what may have been?

How many times will this nostalgia begin an onslaught of dreams,
Of reunification, and happiness ever after?
And to he who thinks, feels, remembers, and dreams as such,
How many times do miracles of this nature come true?

How many? One? Ten in a million? Pipe dream?
Is it all impossible?
Is it all a dream?
How many times does he ask himself this?
How many times?

And if he were to meet her again,
Would he have the courage to fulfill his side of this grand fantasy?
Would he really call out her name,
Run to her with open joy and hold her firmly as if to never lose her again,
Or would he lack the nerve to make such display of inner emotions public?

How many times does he fail his side of the fantasy,
The dream, the hope, the wish, before she has even a chance?
How many times does he feel he will never love another as he loved her?

How many times does he face the reality of her nonexistence in his life
And feel the pain of knowing it may never be the same again?
How many times can he jump from one to another and another,
Yet another and always come up empty-handed
Because it is she he is searching out and never finding in others.
How many times can he compromise who he wants with who he can get?
How many times can he want to call her, or even make the call
And be thwarted, and still maintain hope?

How many times does she think of him, if ever?
How many times does he get the chance to ask
"May we try again, my beautiful friend?"

How many times will I tell you "I love you"
Without letting you hear me?

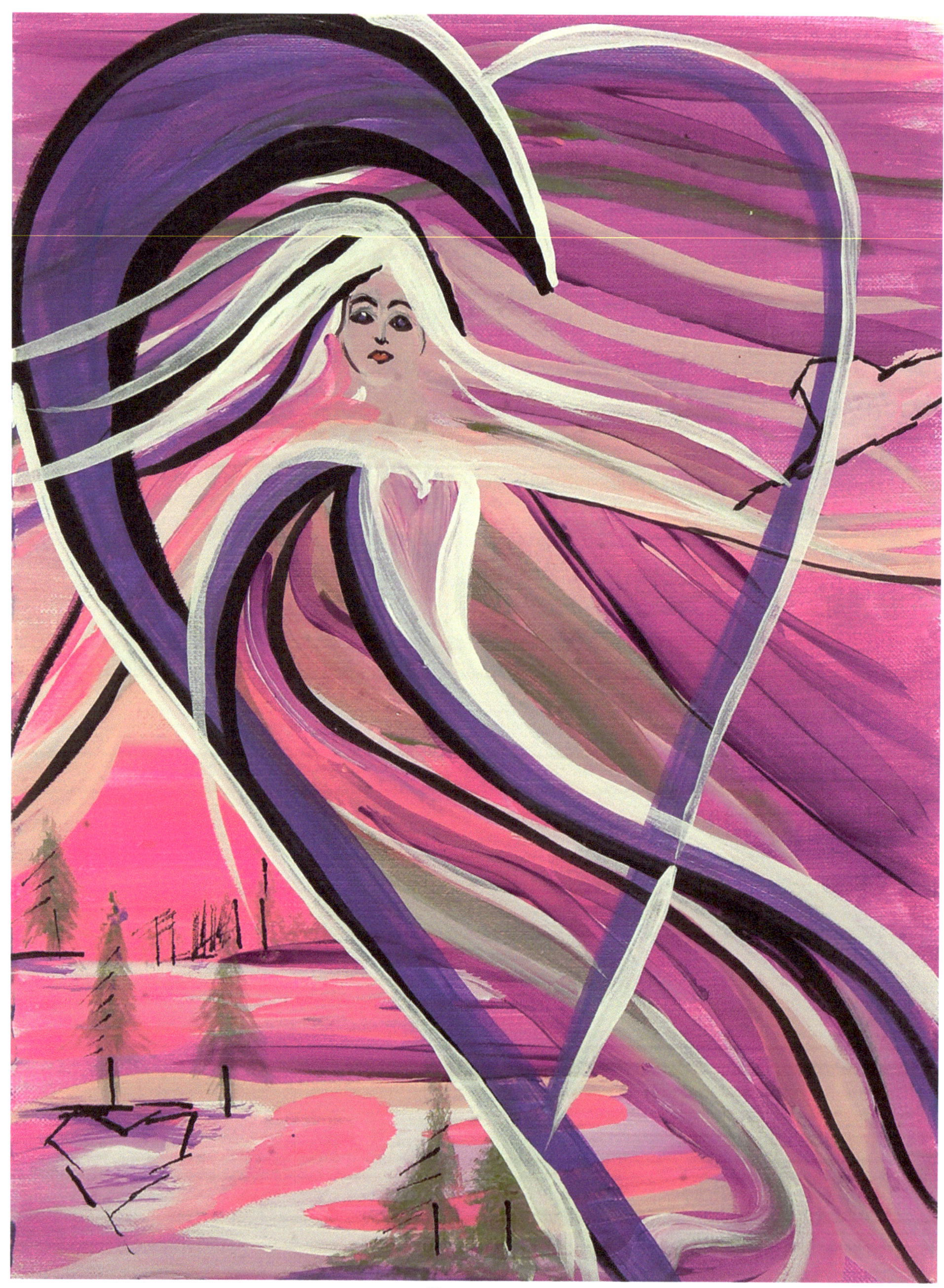

Love

Love

She stands alone above the forest
Somewhere in people's minds.
Barren, defaced, crippled before the world,
A symbol, not living or thinking.

Her life drains from her,
As water from a mountain spring.
The calm of evening does nothing for her,
Neither does the soft, cool night.

Waving in the evening light
It is as if she never existed,
Merely an image in my head.

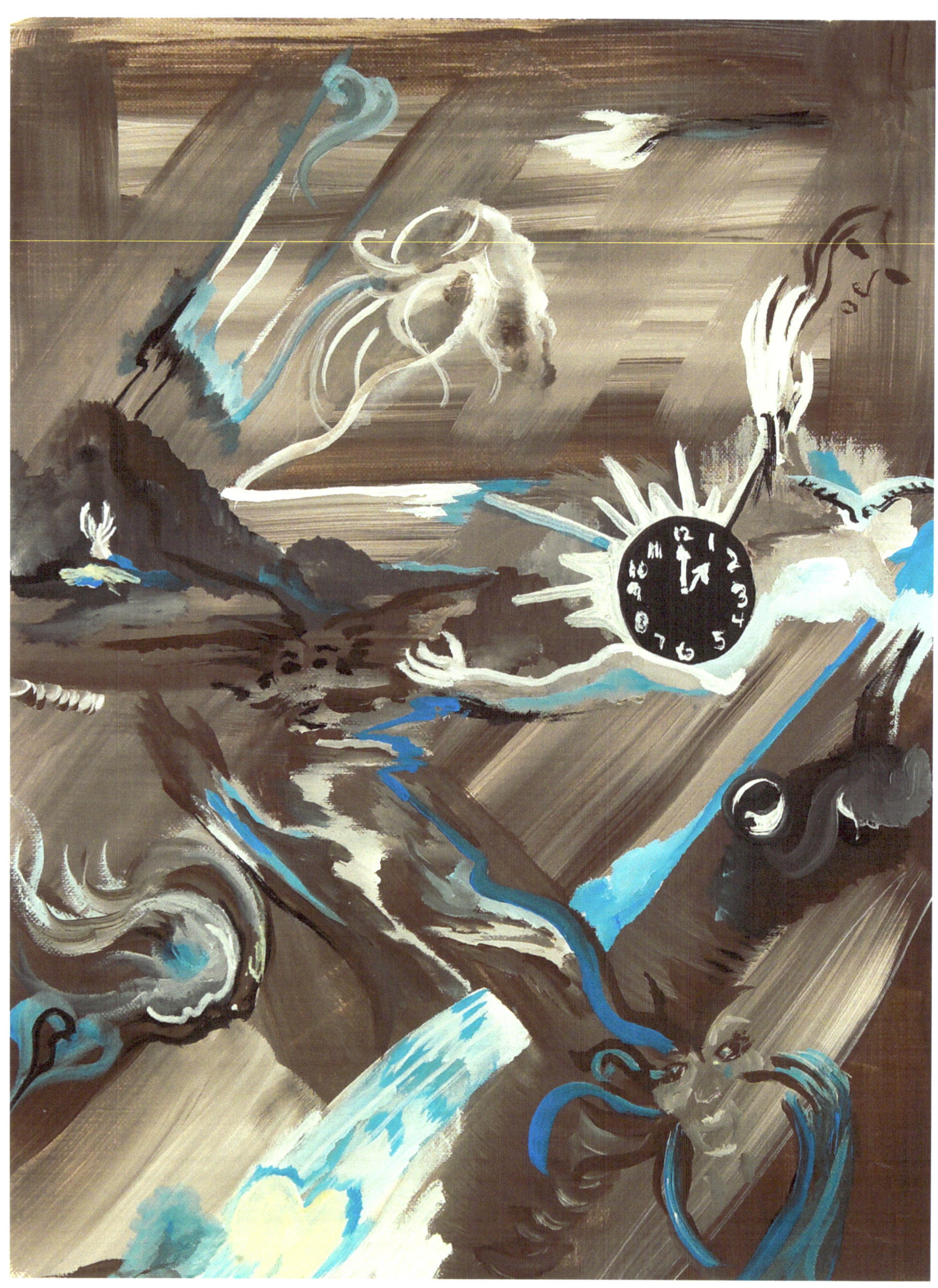

Wounded

Wounded

Dream of the past with all its glory
Make of it what you like.
Think of what might have been, and
Shape it for your pleasure.

Someday I want to be known for insight,
Someday I hope to be a recognized talent,
Someday I need to find love.
Somedays never come.

The years I have wasted are precious
Lost to the cruel magnet of time.
How many lie before me?
Will I be as careless as before?

People, I climb a mountain.
No one sees my accomplishment.

Children, I play a game.
You are unmoved.

Mother, I cry out for you.
You really do not hear me.

Father, I reach for you.
You are outside my grasp.

Sister, I need your tender touch.
I cannot feel.

Lover, I want your healing love.
My wounds need more than that.

When you lose touch with yourself,
There is but one way to regroup.
Discover answers within yourself
And make peace with yourself.

You will not be respected as you desire until you do.

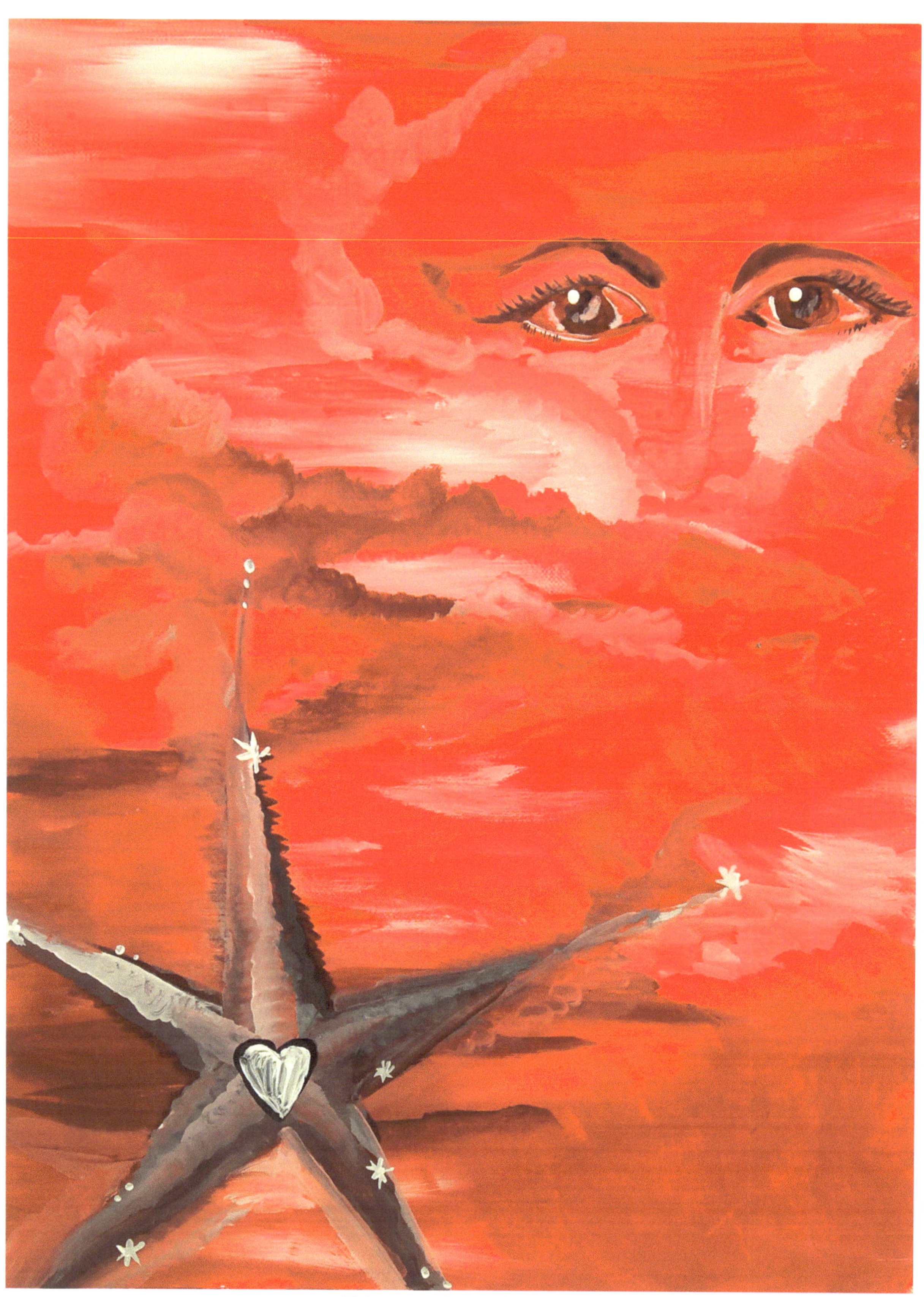

Rivers of the Soul

Rivers of the Soul

Revel in that touch of mystic melancholy to life,
surreal as the space in time before a spring shower
with the dance and aroma of fresh new leaves'
unhurried flight from the fingers of a gentle breeze.

We feel that longing for love and affection,
not relegated to one person, one being, nor one entity.
The urge for the admiration, adoration, even lust of another.

The unthinkable needs one loves to think about,
To grasp in the heart, mind and soul,
To experience with unending majesty and mastery.

Leaves fondled and caressed
are background to sensuous aromas of flowers
scenting this world of timeless magic.
Cool hands of winsome winds
wrap lightly around the waist, arms and inner soul,
lightly, ever so lightly reaching deeper and deeper,
down to depths where no labels are found,
no benchmarks for having been trod upon
or reached by any living soul.

Down to the innermost desires and longings,
Down to the world where all is sinfully obscure,
where a wisp of that winsome breeze can bring forth
a response from our inmost sensual feelings.

Not a feeling that can be explained,
but only entertained as part of life.
This feeling cannot be called upon to manifest itself.
A feeling as such can only ebb and flow with the
emotion one possesses in the rivers of one's soul.

These rivers are so awesome in scope as to absolutely defy description.
We make up words, names and marks,
brands to burn into our hearts to describe what we feel,
but, as a brand on an animal, it only covers part of the property.
The brand becomes a black mark on a good, true and innocent fact of life.

"Love" is not owned by those four letters –
They imprison it.
Trapped and placed into small minds as an excuse for things to happen,
a reason for the insanities of this troubled world.
"Love" is nothing but a four-letter brand on life without corporal existence.
It covers only part of the truth,
so insignificant a part as to be meaningless
to the true essence for which it stands.

Ah, yes, the rivers of our souls are to be found in contemplation,
explored in silent, magical moments,
heard and smelled and lusted after with passionate fury –
seen and felt and experienced –
a mere touch of the softest finger of the wind –
the slightest hint of perfumed scent in the air –
the sheer terror of emotional imbalance.

Labels do nothing more than mar
a feeling, a life dream.
This world was never so beautiful
as at the moment of awareness.

Rivers of the soul – so uncharted, so neglected,
so foolishly stigmatized over the eons –
dare anyone to challenge them,
to do more than inspect and judge them.

They challenge everyone to explore more than themselves,
to see more than they can see, to hear, smell, touch more
than is possible in our world of labels and names and brands on life.

Swim in the river of your inner soul,
the dark, murky current that sweeps you to places you could never reach on your own.
Feel the immensity and power of longing for more insight
into a world we are totally ill-equipped to explore.

Take that plunge down, down, down, down down, down, down,
past the tingle in your spine, down, down, down, down, down,
past T. S. Elliot's "we are the hollow men, we are the
stuffed men …", down, down, down, down, down,
into the oblivion of that tumultuous ocean of passion
and lust and longing and truth.

Oh, that chaotic truth that we are nothing.
We are only bottles that house so potent an elixir
that we fear as much what is inside us as outside.
Keep going if you dare,
down, down, down, down, down, down, down, down,
past the questions of life's relevancy,
of whether or not to end it,
of how to keep your sanity,
past suicide as the only recourse to this unsolvable maze.
Pause only at death being the only absolute in living.

So many currents, so many streams, so many directions to explore.
Oh, what I'd give to have one who could see this,
one who could step in and ride this misty voyage into the blackest of horizons,
someone to feel horrified by an honest look into the truth of the rivers of the soul,
someone to bed down in the blackest of mists,
in the most evasive and intruding of eternity's conception,
someone to understand the complete and total lust of forever.

Oh, for someone to see that the rivers of the soul
are so much more intricate than limitless space,
so compressed and dense and eternally boundless
as compared with the almost empty realm of space itself.

We hold this within us, this world, this universe,
this inconceivable of all possible worlds.
Yet no one can see it, hear it, smell it.

Experience and explore the rivers of your soul.
In our realities there are only labels and names,
fighting and wars, crime and corruption.
Which world would you rather be in?

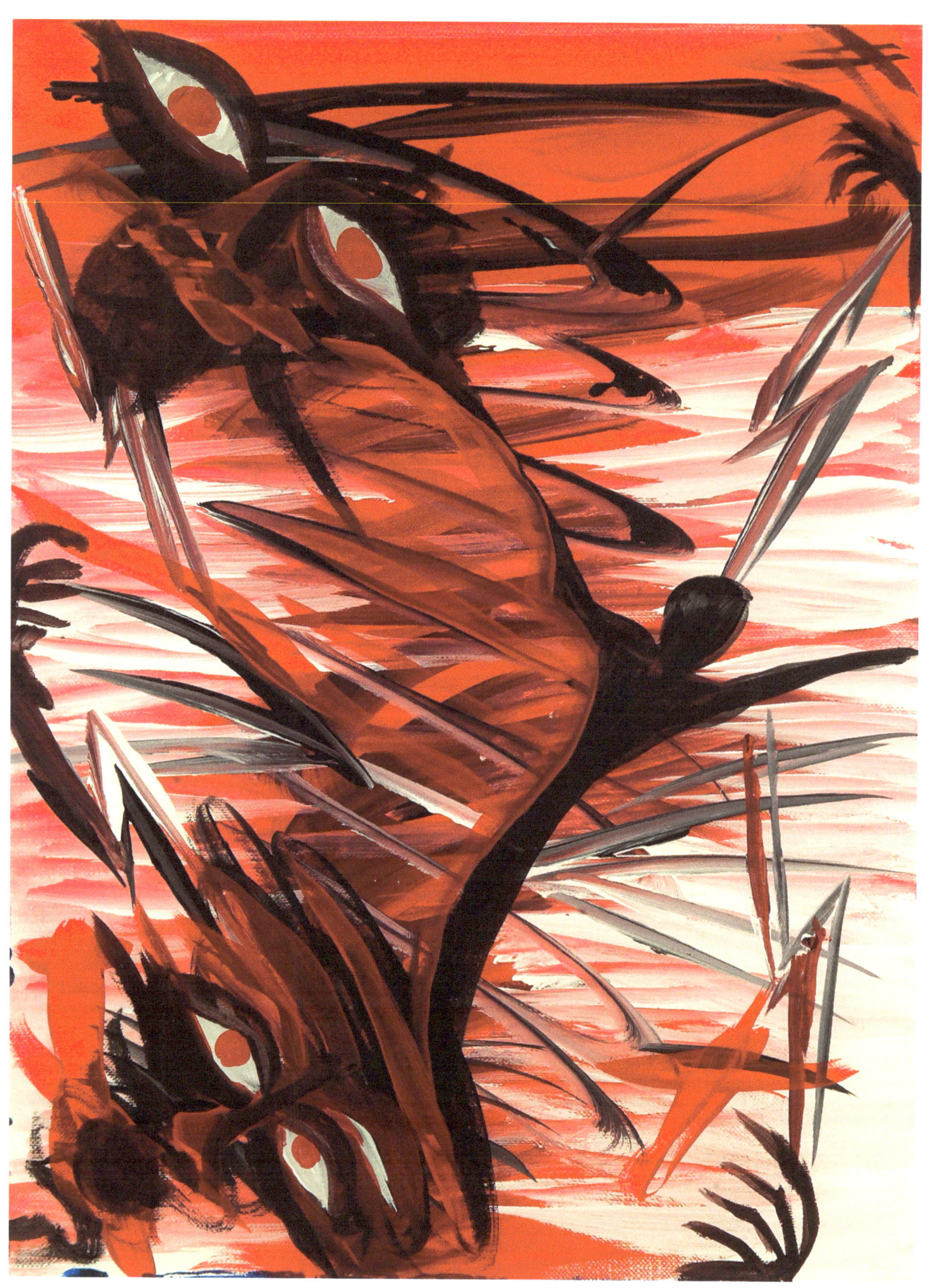

Anger

Anger.

So volatile,

White-hot and quick.

So prevalent, so nasty,

So heated, so sick.

Eating away morsels of life.

Destroying the warmth of relaxation,

Blinding the eyes from a beautiful world,

Sinking the heart in a quagmire of self-importance.

Hell burns the hole, furious and infected,

Through nerves and blood vessels interconnected,

Through stomach and head, simultaneously careless

Of the health and the wealth of all that is good.

Anger bankrupts the soul of rich, noble thought.

Anger reaches for sanity in the waning moments of reason,

Anger feeds on the trouble it has wrought.

Hell has its place – let's keep it off Earth.

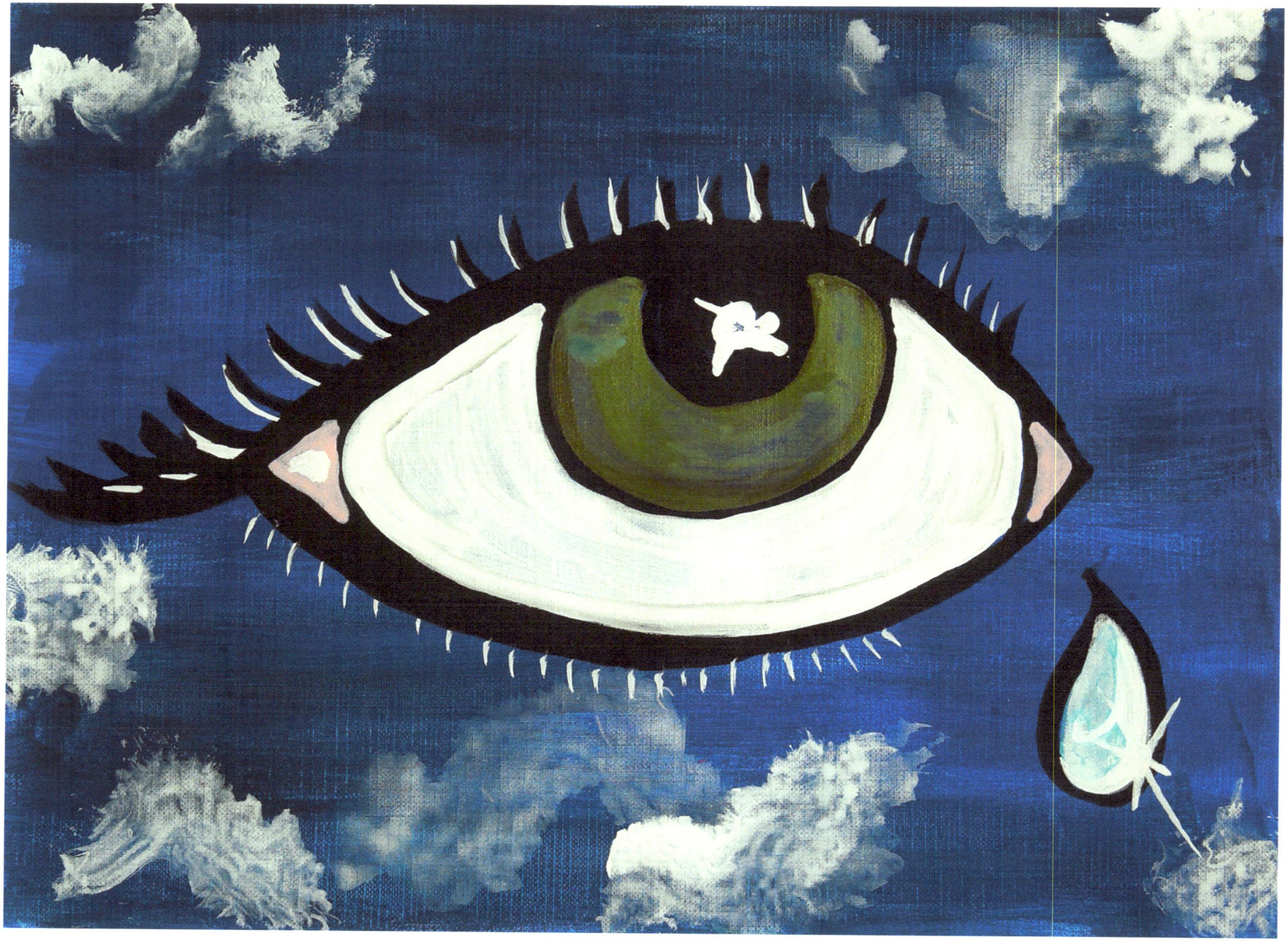

Did She Ever Care?

Did She Ever Care?

Did she look to the light
In the blackness of the evening?
Did she long for the hand
That would treat her right?

Does she cry for the loss
Of the one who wanted her?
Will she ever regret
She threw me away?

I am gone now,
Left for peace of mind.
I am strong now,
The dream left behind.

But every time I sleep,
Every time I close my eyes,
I ask myself,
Will she ever miss my love? Did she ever hear me cry?

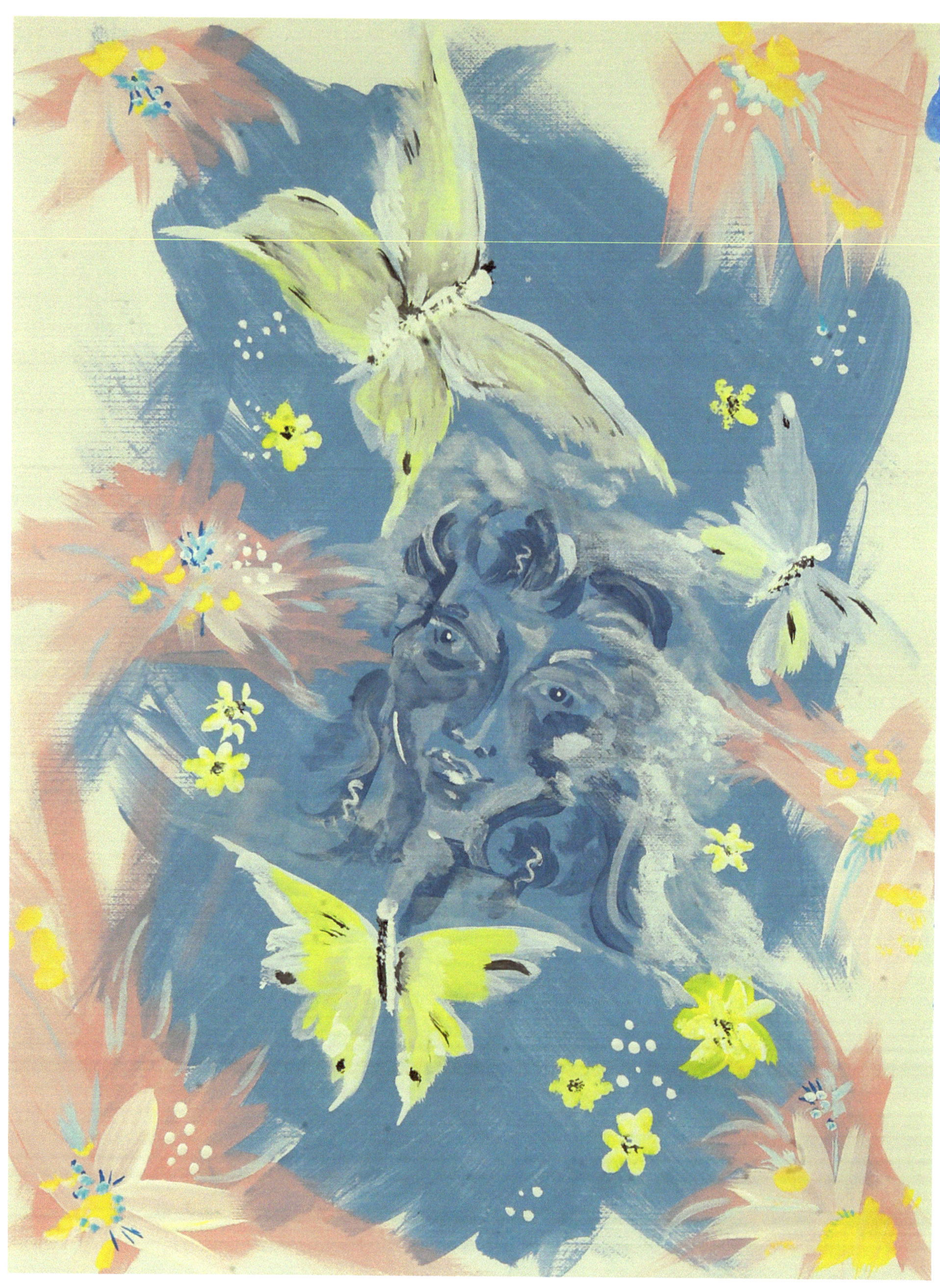

Until I Was Alone

Until I Was Alone

Ripples like a thousand faces
Blur reflections of the evening forest
Trees shimmer in faded light
Remind me of a dream

I used to sit by my lover's side
On the banks of Shelley Lake
I'd tell her of my wildest dreams
And chances I would take

We laughed and played while the sun was up
I never heard the sound
Of discord or unhappiness
Until I was alone

Oh, I see my love in the evening water
A glistening ripple of days gone by
I'll stay here until darkness falls,
Count every breath I take
Sit among the darkened trees
And cry in Shelley Lake

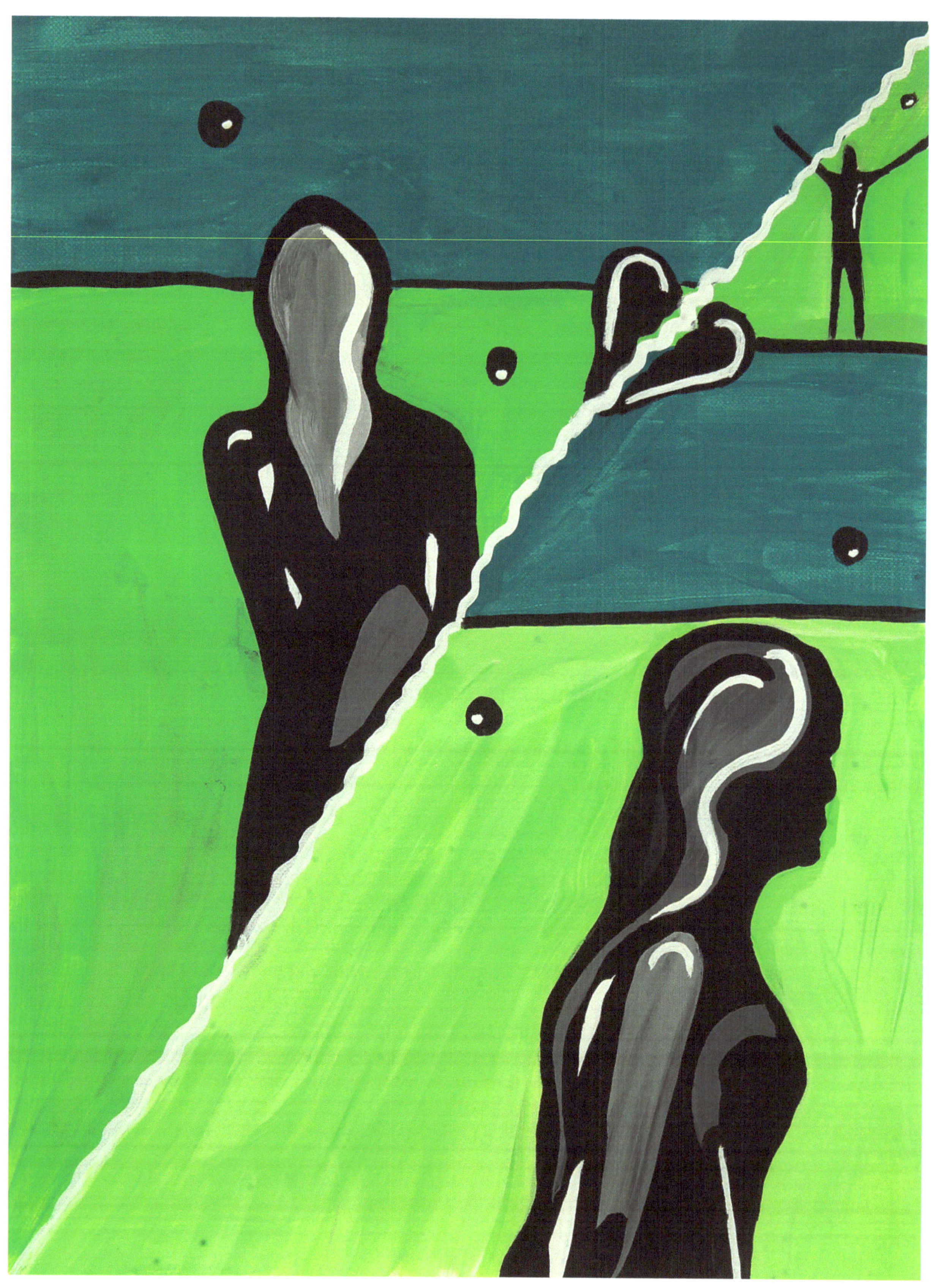

Precious Gift

Precious Gift

The day woman no longer sees me,
When I am but one of a conglomerate,
Commanding no positive thought in any form,
Life has lost its meaning.

I live so that she may have life,
Dream so her wishes may come true,
Endure so her pain might be diminished.
I love so that she may be loved.

A woman's most valued gift is herself;
Her thoughts, her companionship, her love.
For what else in life is more precious?

Is it not the same for men?

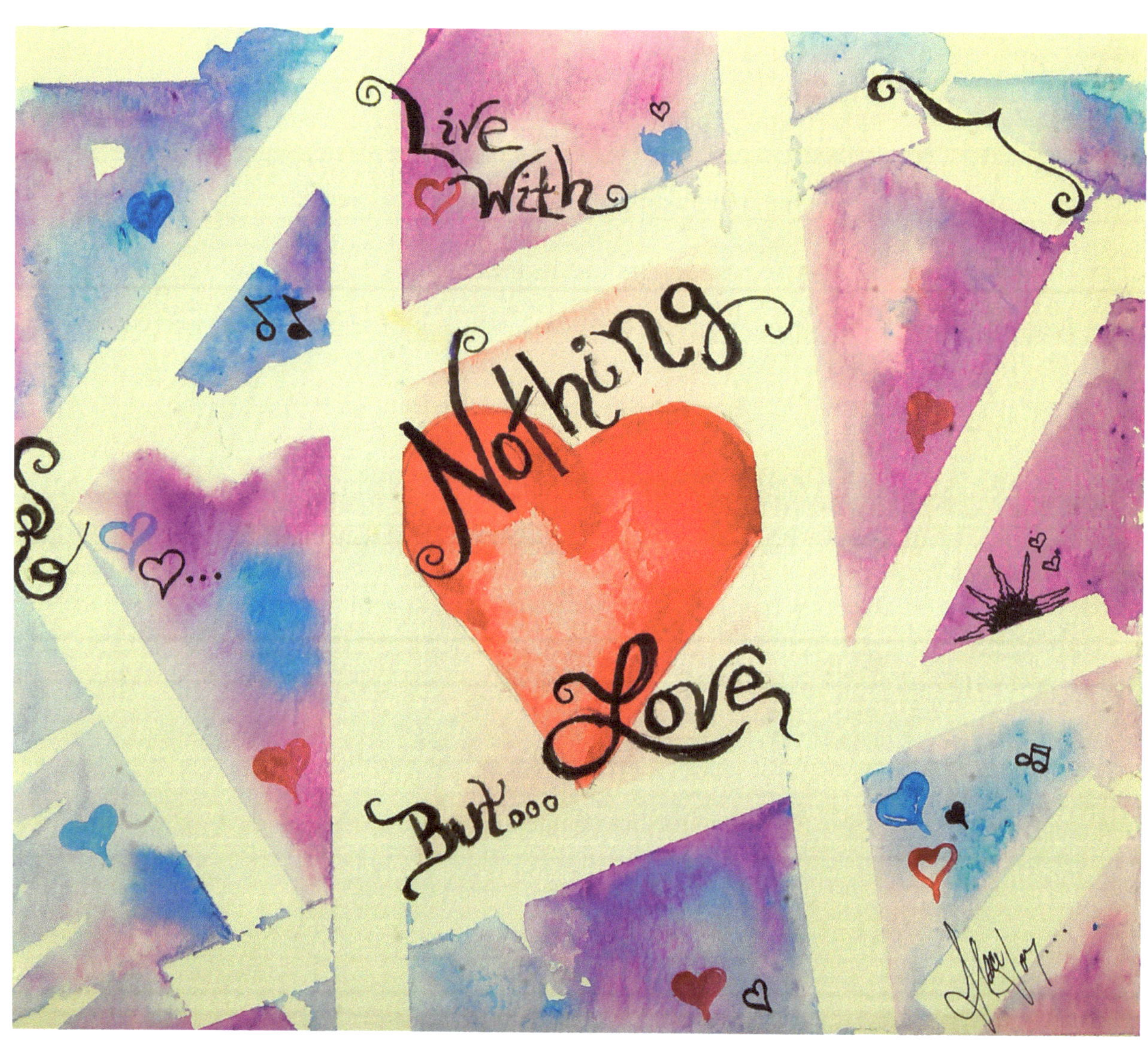
Live With
Nothing
But...
Love

About the Author

Michael Ray King grew up in a small town in West Virginia. The first twenty-two years of his life were spent in the lovely mountains of his home state. Upon graduation from college in 1981 he moved to Raleigh, North Carolina, where he lived for the next seventeen years. It was in Raleigh that he met his wife, Bobbie.

Michael and Bobbie have six children, ranging from toddler to adulthood. In 1998 Michael relocated his family to Florida, and is now living in Palm Coast.

While basketball, bicycling and writing are some of his passions, it is his love of mountains that will someday carry him back there. He loves snow skiing with one of his daughters and plays basketball with his youngest son regularly. Bobbie and two of his daughters love horseback riding, and one day the family aspires to have a rural home with horses, dogs and crackling fireplaces. Long walks on crisp autumn days are some of Michael's favorite times.

Michael is currently working on a book for the Joy & Care Giving Foundation, a nonprofit organization that is building much-needed schools and libraries in the Philippines. Helping children is high on his list of priorities. He coaches his youngest son's basketball team and continues to learn how to be the best father he can be.

His book, *Fatherhood 101: Bonding Tips for Building Loving Relationships*, was his first foray into helping other fathers realize their potential. He currently has plans to expand this work over a broad spectrum of the fatherhood experience.

Michael is a member of the Rogues Gallery Writers, the Professional Writers Group and the Florida Writers Association. He is also the Vice President of Education at Coastmasters, the local Toastmasters affiliate to Palm Coast.

He is available for speaking engagements and discussions on the topics of fatherhood, writing, and publishing. He may be contacted at author@michaelrayking.com.

Also by Michael Ray King

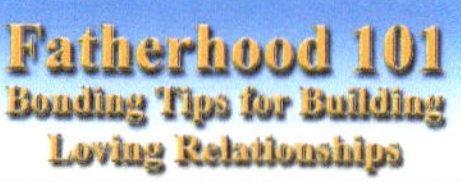

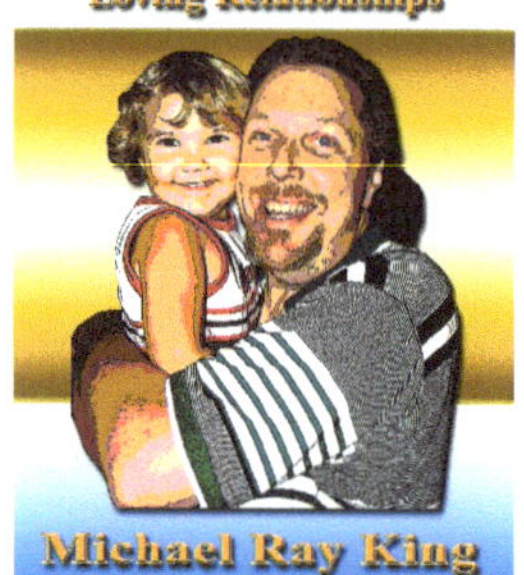

Fatherhood 101: Bonding Tips for Building Loving Relationships
Published by ClearView Press Inc.
PO Box 353431
Palm Coast, FL 32135-3431
386-290-6908
http://www.fatherhood-101.com
http://www.clearviewpressinc.com

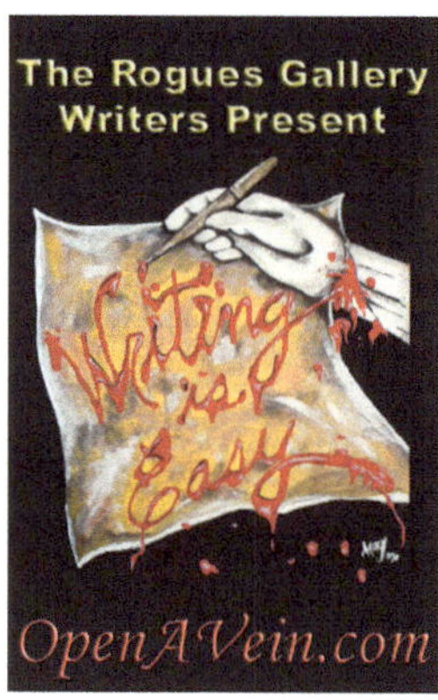

Writing is Easy – Open A Vein
Published by ClearView Press Inc.
PO Box 353431
Palm Coast, FL 32135-3431
386-290-6908
http://www.writingiseasy.com
http://www.clearviewpressinc.com

About the Artist/Illustrator

Tracy McDurmon, aka Tracy Panthera, is a Florida girl. She is a divorced mother of two awesome boys, Kasey and Dalton, who are the reasons she rolls out of bed and stays strong each day. Tracy lives life like it is the only one she has, and from time to time gets off track like anyone else. She cherishes each great friend who has helped with her journey.

Tracy loves the beach, the arts, and the metaphysical. With open heart and mind she explores all the wonderful experiences that cross her path. She loves to fish and has a passion for writing as well. Her work is considered fantasy and unusual for the unusual minded. She believes in allowing her imagination to go wild! She wishes love and light to everyone she meets and encourages us to enjoy the ride. Tracy can be found on the web at www.TracyMcdurmon.com.

www.ingramcontent.com/pod-product-compliance
Ingram Content Group UK Ltd.
Pitfield, Milton Keynes, MK11 3LW, UK
UKHW060120300726
14090UKWH00002B/287

9780979962318